Mysterious Waters

Mysterious Waters

BERMUDA'S ENIGMA UNVEILED

Olivia K.

Spectra Enterprise

Contents

Table Of Content

Chapter 8: The Human Element

Chapter 9: Beyond Borders

Introduction

Strange Waters: Bermuda's Conundrum Disclosed

The Bermuda Triangle, a stretch of sea settled between Bermuda, Florida, and Puerto Rico, has long caught the creative mind of mariners, researchers, and connivance scholars the same. In the dark blue scope of the Atlantic, stories of evaporated ships, baffling peculiarities, and unexplained vanishings have woven an embroidery of secret around this cryptic district. As we set out on the excursion to disclose the privileged insights of these baffling waters, we end up on a mission to isolate reality from fiction and shed light on the bewildering charm of the Bermuda Triangle.

Wandering into the void of the Bermuda Triangle, one is promptly stood up to with a rich embroidery of verifiable records and incredible stories that have added to its persona. The Alarms' Call, so to speak, draws us into a domain where oceanic legends interlaces with the real world. Mariners from times gone past discussed shocking lights, unusual sounds, and spooky specters tormenting the waters. Such legendary components, while charming, act as the setting against which the Bermuda Triangle's real essence is covered in vagueness.

Evaporating Acts, the peculiarity that has given the Bermuda Triangle its unfavorable standing, unfurls a story of mysterious vanishings that have made a permanent imprint on the locale's set of experiences. The chronicles of oceanic records are stained with records of boats and airplane evaporating suddenly. From the spooky vanishing of Flight 19 out of 1945 to the later occurrences including current vessels, the Bermuda Triangle's inclination for making the unexplainable a the truth is a string that winds around its way through time.

As we dig further, we wear the Logical Focal point to examine the overarching speculations that look to demystify the Bermuda Triangle. Normal clarifications proliferate, from attractive irregularities influencing route instruments to methane hydrate emissions causing abrupt sinkings. Land highlights, frequently ignored, become the point of convergence of conversations as we disentangle the privileged insights of the profound. The apparently powerful events find establishing in the logical domain, testing the idea that the Bermuda Triangle is a paranormal vortex.

Mysteries of the Profound coax us to investigate the sea floor's secret marvels and expected influence on boats and planes. Unknown regions underneath the waves hold land developments that could impact route and security. The investigation of these remote ocean riddles is a demonstration of the intricacy of the submerged world, where the transaction of structural powers and maritime flows might hold the way to understanding the secrets that have frustrated us for a really long time.

Connivances Above water acquaints us with the shadowy universe of fear inspired notions that whirl around the Bermuda Triangle. From extraterrestrial contribution to supposed government concealments, these hypotheses have formed public insight and energized the flames of hypothesis. Unwinding reality from the fiction requires an insightful eye, as we explore through the cloudy waters of falsehood and think about the impact of media emotionalism on the formation of the Bermuda Triangle fantasy.

Exploring the Obscure leads us through the verifiable points of view on route difficulties in the locale. Early adventurers confronted the overwhelming assignment of diagramming unknown waters, depending on simple instruments and heavenly route. Innovative progressions have since changed route, yet the Bermuda Triangle stays a proving ground for mariners and pilots the same. Understanding the advancement of route reveals insight into the intrinsic difficulties presented by the area's one of a kind qualities.

The Human Component comes to the front as we look at the job of human mistake in occurrences inside the Bermuda Triangle. While the charm of extraordinary clarifications enamors the creative mind, a more critical glance at the occurrences uncovers an example of missteps, misinterpretations, and mental blunders. Accounts of endurance arise, offering a human viewpoint on the difficulties looked by the individuals who have crossed the baffling waters and lived to tell the story.

Past Lines widens our viewpoint by inspecting worldwide perspectives on the Bermuda Triangle. Various societies offer their own understandings and strange notions that might be of some value, adding to the different woven artwork of convictions encompassing the area. Investigating these social subtleties permits us to see the value in the worldwide interest with the Bermuda Triangle and how its secrets rise above geological limits.

As we approach the zenith of our excursion, Divulging the Riddle unites the strings of examination, exposing legends, and introducing a far reaching perspective on the Bermuda Triangle. The logical, verifiable, and human components combine to offer a nuanced comprehension of the locale's secrets. While the charm of the obscure remaining parts, a fair point of view arises — one that recognizes the Bermuda Triangle's enrapturing history yet scatters the shadows of dread and vulnerability.

All in all, Secretive Waters: Bermuda's Puzzle Disclosed is a journey into the core of one of the world's most prominent secrets. Through investigation, examination, and a promise to unwinding reality, we explore the turbulent waters of hypothesis and show up at a more clear comprehension of the Bermuda Triangle. This conundrum, when saturated with fantasy and dread, uncovers itself as a juncture of normal peculiarities, human elements, and the getting through charm of the unexplored world.

Chapter 1

Into the Abyss

Into the Pit

The excursion into the mysterious domain of the Bermuda Triangle starts with a pondering look into the limitlessness of the Atlantic Sea, where the directions of Bermuda, Florida, and Puerto Rico converge to make a three-sided fix of water that has gathered a standing saturated with secret and interest. As we set out on this investigation, it is fundamental to perceive that the Bermuda Triangle, otherwise called Satan's Triangle, is a district that has enamored the human creative mind for a really long time, filling in as the background for various stories of disappeared ships, lost airplane, and mysterious peculiarities.

The name "Into the Pit" embodies the quintessence of our undertaking — a dive into the profundities of verifiable records, unbelievable stories, and the shared perspective that has formed the impression of the Bermuda Triangle. The riddle is complex, woven from strings of legend and reality, and as we explore these dinky waters, we experience a heap of stories that have filled the charm of the district.

The Alarms' Call, the primary section of our investigation, submerges us in the legendary viewpoints encompassing the Bermuda Triangle. Mariners and adventurers of past times discussed frightful lights, baffling sounds, and spooky spirits that appeared to oppose clarification. These stories, went down through ages, cast a spell on the district, adding to its standing as where the ordinary principles of reality appear to disentangle. The impact of sea legends makes way for our excursion, accentuating the entwining of fantasy and reality that portrays the Bermuda Triangle's persona.

Disappearing Acts, the subsequent part, uncovers the focal topic that has given the Bermuda Triangle its unpropitious standing. The verifiable record is damaged with records of boats and airplane vanishing suddenly, abandoning just inquiries and hypothesis. Maybe the most notorious episode is the vanishing of Flight 19 out of 1945, a group of U.S. Naval force planes that disappeared during a preparation flight. The quest and salvage mission for Flight 19 itself turned out to be essential for the Bermuda Triangle legend when the salvage airplane additionally vanished.

The section investigates other remarkable vanishings, both verifiable and contemporary, making a story that intensifies the feeling of secret encompassing the locale.

The Logical Focal point, our third section, fills in as a basic device in our investigation. Here, we dive into the logical speculations that look to demystify the Bermuda Triangle. Normal clarifications proliferate, going from attractive inconsistencies that could impede route instruments to the arrival of methane hydrates causing abrupt and unforeseen sinkings. Topography turns into a point of convergence of conversation as we examine the effect of submerged developments on the locale's elements. By taking on a logical viewpoint, we expect to carry lucidity to peculiarities frequently covered in hypothesis and fables.

Insider facts of the Profound, our fourth section, welcomes us to investigate the sea depths' secret miracles and their possible effect on the secrets of the Bermuda Triangle. Unknown domains underneath the waves hold land arrangements that could affect route and wellbeing. As we explore the profundities, the conversation reaches out to the submerged world's intricacy, stressing the interaction of structural powers, maritime flows, and the geographical scene as contributing variables to the conundrum that has baffled travelers and researchers the same.

Connivances Above water, the fifth section, pulls back the drape on the shadowy universe of paranoid notions that twirl around the Bermuda Triangle. Extraterrestrial inclusion, claimed government smoke screens, and paranormal peculiarities become the dominant focal point as we explore through the domain of emotionalism and hypothesis. Disentangling reality from the fiction turns into a difficult undertaking, requiring an insightful eye and a basic assessment of the impact of media drama on the creation and propagation of the Bermuda Triangle fantasy.

Exploring the Obscure, our 6th part, guides us through authentic viewpoints on route difficulties inside the Bermuda Triangle. Early wayfarers confronted the overwhelming undertaking of outlining unknown waters, depending on simple apparatuses and heavenly route. Mechanical progressions have changed route, yet the Bermuda Triangle stays a proving ground for mariners and pilots the same. Understanding the advancement of route reveals insight into the inborn difficulties presented by the area's extraordinary attributes.

The Human Component, our seventh section, delivers the job of human blunder in occurrences inside the Bermuda Triangle. While the charm of heavenly clarifications enamors the creative mind, a more critical gander at the episodes uncovers an example of errors, confusions, and failures to understand the situation. Accounts of endurance arise, offering a human point of view on the difficulties looked by the individuals who have navigated the puzzling waters and lived to tell the story. This part fills in as an update that, in the midst of the persona, human elements assume a huge part in the story of the Bermuda Triangle.

Past Boundaries, the eighth section, widens our viewpoint by looking at global perspectives on the Bermuda Triangle. Various societies offer their translations and odd notions that might be of some value, adding to the assorted embroidery of convictions encompassing the area. Investigating these social subtleties permits us to see the value in the worldwide interest with the Bermuda Triangle and how its secrets rise above geological limits.

As we approach the finish of our excursion, Uncovering the Puzzle, our 10th part, unites the strings of examination, exposing legends, and introducing a far reaching perspective on the Bermuda Triangle. The logical, verifiable, and human components join to offer a nuanced comprehension of the locale's secrets. While the charm of the obscure remaining parts, a fair viewpoint arises — one that recognizes the Bermuda Triangle's dazzling history however dissipates the shadows of dread and vulnerability. The conundrum that once appeared to be inconceivable now uncovers itself as a conjunction of normal peculiarities, human variables, and the getting through charm of the unexplored world.

All in all, the endeavor Into the Pit fills in as a complete investigation of the Bermuda Triangle, unwinding its secrets and revealing insight into the multi-layered nature of this confounding district. This excursion crosses through the domains of legend and reality, science and hypothesis, giving a comprehensive comprehension that rises above the limits of famous stories. The Bermuda Triangle, while keeping a demeanor of persona, turns out to be more agreeable, its insider facts uncovered from the perspective of investigation and request.

1.1 Introduction to the Bermuda Triangle's mystique.

Prologue to the Bermuda Triangle's Persona

In the immense territory of the Atlantic Sea, between the places of Bermuda, Florida, and Puerto Rico, lies a three-sided district that has for quite some time been inseparable from secret and interest — the Bermuda Triangle. As we leave on an excursion to unwind the persona encompassing this perplexing region, it is fundamental to recognize that the Bermuda Triangle has turned into an image of interest, dread, and hypothesis. Its name brings out stories of evaporated ships, lost airplane, and unexplained peculiarities that have caught the human creative mind for quite a long time.

The appeal of the Bermuda Triangle is well established in verifiable records that date back to the Time of Investigation. Early mariners talked about unusual events, for example, compasses failing and frightful lights not too far off, as they explored the slippery waters inside the limits of the triangle. These stories, went down through ages, established the groundwork for the persona that would later become inseparable from the area. The idea of a reviled or tormented ocean got forward movement, making an emanation of vulnerability that penetrated sea legend.

As we dive into the core of the Bermuda Triangle's persona, we experience the principal part of our investigation — The Alarms' Call. This allegorical call allures us to investigate the legendary viewpoints encompassing the locale, where oceanic fables entwines with the real world. Mariners from past times related experiences with spooky phantoms, unusual sounds, and unexplained lights that appeared to resist the laws of nature. These accounts, frequently excused as results of creative mind, set up for the rise of the Bermuda Triangle as a spot where the common changes into the exceptional.

Evaporating Acts, the second part in our story, uncovers the center component that has energized the Bermuda Triangle's foreboding standing. The verifiable record is overflowing with records of boats and airplane vanishing suddenly, abandoning a path of secret and hypothesis. Maybe the most famous occurrence is the vanishing of Flight 19 of every 1945 — a group of U.S. Naval force planes that evaporated during a normal preparation flight. The resulting search and salvage mission likewise met a puzzling destiny, adding to the persevering through story of the Bermuda Triangle as a position of incomprehensible vanishings.

The Logical Focal point, our third part, fills in as a crucial device in our journey to comprehend the Bermuda Triangle's secrets. Here, we examine the different logical hypotheses that have been proposed to demystify the district. Regular clarifications, going from attractive irregularities influencing route instruments to geographical arrangements affecting the sea floor, are analyzed exhaustively. The logical focal point offers an offset to the supernatural stories, testing the impression of the Bermuda Triangle as a paranormal vortex.

Insider facts of the Profound, our fourth section, prompts us to investigate the sea floor's secret marvels and their possible impact on the district's secrets. Strange domains underneath the waves hold topographical developments that could influence route and wellbeing. As we explore these profundities, the conversation stretches out to the intricacy of the submerged world, where structural powers, submerged flows, and geographical highlights combine to establish a climate that is both lovely and possibly perilous.

Schemes Above water, the fifth section, lifts the shroud on the domain of paranoid fears that have woven themselves into the texture of Bermuda Triangle legend. Extraterrestrial contribution, government smoke screens, and paranormal peculiarities become the overwhelming focus as we explore through the domain of emotionalism and hypothesis. Unwinding reality from the fiction turns into a perplexing undertaking, requiring an insightful eye and a basic assessment of the impact of media emotionalism on the creation and propagation of the Bermuda Triangle fantasy.

Exploring the Obscure, our 6th section, guides us through authentic points of view on route difficulties inside the Bermuda Triangle. Early pioneers confronted the overwhelming errand of diagramming unfamiliar waters, depending on simple apparatuses and heavenly route. Mechanical headways have changed route, yet the Bermuda Triangle stays a proving ground for mariners and pilots the same. Understanding the development of route reveals insight into the inborn difficulties presented by the district's remarkable qualities.

The Human Component, our seventh section, delivers the job of human blunder in episodes inside the Bermuda Triangle. While the charm of powerful clarifications enamors the creative mind, a more critical glance at the occurrences uncovers an example of errors, misconceptions, and failures to understand the situation. Accounts of endurance arise, offering a human point of view on the difficulties looked by the individuals who have crossed the baffling waters and lived to tell the story. This section fills in as an update that, in the midst of the persona, human variables assume a huge part in the story of the Bermuda Triangle.

Past Boundaries, our eighth section, expands our viewpoint by analyzing global perspectives on the Bermuda Triangle. Various societies offer their translations and strange notions that might be of some value, adding to the different embroidery of convictions encompassing the area. Investigating these social subtleties permits us to see the value in the worldwide interest with the Bermuda Triangle and how its secrets rise above geological limits.

As we approach the climax of our excursion, Revealing the Riddle, our 10th part, unites the strings of examination, exposing fantasies, and introducing an exhaustive perspective on the Bermuda Triangle. The logical, verifiable, and human components merge to offer a nuanced comprehension of the district's secrets. While the charm of the obscure remaining parts, a reasonable viewpoint arises — one that recognizes the Bermuda Triangle's spellbinding history however scatters the shadows of dread and vulnerability.

The puzzler that once appeared to be outlandish now uncovers itself as an intersection of normal peculiarities, human variables, and the getting through charm of the unexplored world.

All in all, our investigation into the presentation of the Bermuda Triangle's persona takes us on a multi-layered venture through history, fables, science, and human experience. The Bermuda Triangle, as opposed to an independently otherworldly substance, arises as a perplexing embroidery woven from different strings of legend and reality. As we explore these complicated waters of hypothesis and request, the persona of the Bermuda Triangle starts to disentangle, uncovering a story that is as much about human interest and creative mind for all intents and purposes about the intrinsic secrets of the normal world.

1.2 Overview of historical disappearances and strange occurrences.

Outline of Authentic Vanishings and Bizarre Events in the Bermuda Triangle

The Bermuda Triangle, a district of the Atlantic Sea known for its baffling standing, has become inseparable from stories of evaporated ships, lost airplane, and weird events that challenge regular clarification. This section fills in as a passage into the core of the Bermuda Triangle's persona by giving a top to bottom outline of verifiable vanishings and exceptional occasions that have added to the puzzle encompassing this three-sided stretch of water.

The chronicles of oceanic history are loaded with records of boats cruising into the Bermuda Triangle and staying away forever. One of the earliest and most confounding episodes traces all the way back to the mid-nineteenth century when the USS Cyclops, a gigantic U.S. Naval force freight transport, vanished without a follow in 1918. The boat, persisting 300 group individuals and a heap of manganese metal, was on the way from Brazil to Baltimore when it evaporated. In spite of broad hunt endeavors, no destruction or trash was at any point found, leaving the destiny of the USS Cyclops covered in secret. This vanishing laid the preparation for the story that the Bermuda Triangle was a dangerous district equipped for gulping down huge vessels.

The mystery kept on developing in the years that followed, arriving at a zenith during the prime of flying. Flight 19, a group of five U.S. Naval force planes, left on a standard preparation mission in December 1945 and broadly evaporated suddenly. The pilots, experienced military pilots, revealed compass breakdowns and became bewildered. Regardless of radio correspondences, the group in the long run vanished, and ensuing hunt and salvage missions experienced baffling disasters, including the vanishing of a salvage plane.

The episode energized the Bermuda Triangle fantasy as well as denoted the start of another period in which the district turned into a point of convergence for sensationalized records of puzzling vanishings.

The late twentieth century saw a progression of occurrences that further energized the persona of the Bermuda Triangle. In 1970, the French tanker SS Rosalie was tracked down afloat in the Atlantic with nobody ready. The boat was completely functional, with dinners arranged and tables set, yet the team had evaporated suddenly. Also, in 1972, the extravagance yacht Black magic was accounted for missing off the bank of Miami regardless of ideal atmospheric conditions. The yacht's vanishing, combined with the absence of pain signals, confounded examiners and added one more layer to the account of odd events inside the Bermuda Triangle.

These authentic vanishings, set apart by the shortfall of destruction and the abrupt evaporating of teams and travelers, have contributed altogether to the persona encompassing the Bermuda Triangle. Hypotheses going from extraterrestrial obstruction to submerged peculiarities have been proposed to make sense of these peculiarities. The absence of substantial proof has permitted hypothesis and creative mind to thrive, making a rich embroidery of fantasies and secrets that keep on spellbinding the public's creative mind.

Abnormal events inside the Bermuda Triangle stretch out past vanishings to incorporate reports of unexplained peculiarities saw by mariners and pilots. Spooky lights moving not too far off, baffling haze banks that apparently emerge out of the blue, and electromagnetic irregularities that impede route hardware have all been accounted for inside the limits of the three-sided locale. While doubters contend that these peculiarities can frequently be credited to regular causes or optical deceptions, the combined impact of such reports adds to the overall sense that the Bermuda Triangle is where the laws of physical science and nature might act in an unexpected way.

As we dig into the authentic embroidery of vanishings and unusual events inside the Bermuda Triangle, it becomes apparent that the area's persona isn't exclusively grounded in substantial proof however is similarly molded by the accounts and legends that have been woven into its story. These stories act as preventative admonitions, advised mariners and pilots about the potential perils that anticipate the individuals who adventure into the obscure waters of the triangle. The Bermuda Triangle, in numerous ways, has turned into an image of the innate secret and unconventionality of the ocean, where the common can change into the exceptional.

The accounts of verifiable vanishings and peculiar events inside the Bermuda Triangle likewise cause to notice the difficulties of exploring this area. Early wayfarers confronted the overwhelming undertaking of diagramming these strange waters without the guide of current innovation.

Navigational devices were simple, and divine route was much of the time the main method for deciding a boat's situation. In such a climate, where compasses could act unusually and where the navigational milestones were scant, the Bermuda Triangle turned into an impressive impediment that tried the abilities and mental fortitude of the people who really considered crossing its waters.

Mechanical progressions in the twentieth century have not totally dissipated the difficulties presented by the Bermuda Triangle. While current vessels and airplane benefit from cutting edge route frameworks and correspondence innovations, the locale stays a proving ground for the strength of these instruments. Reports of navigational oddities endure, with some ascribing them to attractive varieties and others hypothesizing about the presence of submerged highlights that disturb traditional route.

The outline of authentic vanishings and unusual events in the Bermuda Triangle features not just the substantial episodes that have astounded examiners yet additionally the elusive feeling of secret that has encircled the district for a really long time. The Bermuda Triangle, as an idea, has risen above its geological limits to turn into an image of the obscure, where the shroud among the real world and the fantastical is slim. The charm of the Bermuda Triangle, molded by authentic occasions and sustained by mainstream society, keeps on bringing the inquisitive and the careful into its strange waters, welcoming investigation, request, and, definitely, further hypothesis.

1.3 Setting the stage for unraveling the enigma.

Making way for Unwinding the Puzzler of the Bermuda Triangle

As we leave on the excursion to unwind the mystery of the Bermuda Triangle, it is basic to set the stage by diving into the verifiable, social, and geological settings that have molded this locale into a baffling and frequently dreaded field. The Bermuda Triangle, arranged in the western piece of the North Atlantic Sea, frames a three-sided limit with vertices at Bermuda, Florida, and Puerto Rico. This geographic design, while apparently harmless, has become inseparable from incomprehensible vanishings, unusual peculiarities, and an unavoidable feeling of the unexplored world.

The persona of the Bermuda Triangle is profoundly interlaced with the authentic accounts that have pervaded sea investigation and maritime undertakings over hundreds of years. Early mariners navigating the Atlantic during the Time of Disclosure confronted impressive difficulties, with the Bermuda Triangle frequently going about as a considerable boundary.

The absence of present day navigational guides, deceptive weather patterns, and the presence of capricious sea flows established a climate where oceanic endeavors were intrinsically unsafe. The seeds of secret were planted as mariners experienced the unforeseen - compasses acting sporadically, abrupt tempests emerging not too far off, and unknown waters testing their navigational ability.

The Bermuda Triangle's charm is additionally uplifted by a rich embroidery of social impacts and oceanic legends. Accounts of apparition ships, otherworldly lights, and legendary ocean animals have been woven into the texture of the district's story, went down through ages of mariners and nautical networks. These stories, frequently grounded in a mix of odd notion and genuine difficulties looked by mariners, add to an air where the everyday can without much of a stretch change into the uncommon. The social scenery encompassing the Bermuda Triangle has made a space where reality and creative mind cross-over, encouraging a climate ready for the development of fantasies and legends.

Navigational difficulties inside the Bermuda Triangle were intensified by the shortfall of solid outlines and the shortage of milestones. Early guides frequently included enormous unfamiliar regions, and mariners, depending on simple instruments and divine route, ended up helpless before flighty sea flows and moving attractive peculiarities. These navigational vulnerabilities established the groundwork for a district laden with danger, where the oceans, on occasion, appeared to hold onto a strange vindictiveness. The verifiable setting, loaded down with the hardships of nautical, makes way for the persevering through persona of the Bermuda Triangle.

Socially, the Bermuda Triangle has become in excess of a geographic locale; it has developed into an image of the obscure and the possibly otherworldly. The combination of geological difficulties, sea history, and social impacts has produced a story that rises above the limits of a particular region on the guide. It is inside this setting that the Bermuda Triangle's mystery unfurls - a conversion of regular peculiarities, mankind's set of experiences, and the consistently present secrets of the sea.

As we set up for unwinding the conundrum, it is fundamental to recognize the vital job of mainstream society in propagating and enhancing the secrets related with the Bermuda Triangle. Books, narratives, and fictionalized accounts have added to the production of a story where the limits among reality and fiction obscure. Prominent episodes, like the vanishing of Flight 19 and the USS Cyclops, have been retold and decorated, further improving the emanation of The Bermuda Triangle as a spot where the conventional principles of the truth are suspended.

The puzzler isn't restricted exclusively to authentic episodes. The Bermuda

Triangle has turned into a material whereupon speculative hypotheses and scheme stories are painted.

Extraterrestrial impedance, submerged irregularities, and government concealments have been proposed as clarifications for the district's secrets. While these hypotheses might need logical approval, they have added layers of intricacy to the puzzle, changing the Bermuda Triangle into a material for hypothesis and discussion.

Geologically, the Bermuda Triangle's quirks stretch out past its vertices. The locale is described by a progression of submerged highlights, including remote ocean channels and an intricate organization of lowered caves. These land arrangements, while fascinating, have additionally energized hypothesis about the potential for submerged peculiarities fit for influencing boats and airplane. The interchange among geography and secret is a urgent part of the Bermuda Triangle's riddle, as it welcomes investigation into the profundities of the sea where endless mysteries might stay covered.

The Inlet Stream, a strong sea momentum moving through the Bermuda Triangle, adds one more layer of intricacy to the district's navigational difficulties. This quick ebb and flow can impact atmospheric conditions, make violent oceans, and possibly add to the quick vanishing of vessels. Understanding the powerful exchange between maritime powers and the novel geology of the Bermuda Triangle is fundamental to disentangling the secrets that have become inseparable from the locale.

In exploring the waters of the Bermuda Triangle's puzzle, it is fundamental to embrace a multidisciplinary approach. Logical request, verifiable investigation, and an appreciation for the social and topographical settings are indispensable parts of the investigation. The Bermuda Triangle is definitely not a static riddle to be tackled; rather, it is a unique interaction of normal powers, human stories, and the never-ending charm of the unexplored world.

Disentangling the mystery of the Bermuda Triangle requires a nuanced understanding that rises above emotionalism and embraces a promise to investigation and revelation. The district's secrets are not only an assortment of unique episodes; they are strings in a bigger embroidery that winds around together the complexities of the sea, the flexibility of human investigation, and the persevering through interest with the mysterious. As we set out on this excursion, the stage is set for a smart and far reaching investigation of the Bermuda Triangle's riddle - a mission to translate the code written in the waves, the breezes, and the profundities of the Atlantic Sea.

In our proceeded with investigation of the Bermuda Triangle's riddle, we dive further into the multi-layered perspectives that set up for understanding the secrets that have covered this district. Past the geological, authentic, and social aspects, the Bermuda Triangle welcomes us to examine the logical speculations, human accounts, and the persevering through charm of the unexplored world.

The logical focal point gives a basic viewpoint in our mission to disentangle the conundrum. While mainstream society frequently inclines towards the thrilling, logical request looks to secure our grasping in observational proof. One pervasive hypothesis sets that the Bermuda Triangle might be exposed to attractive abnormalities. Attractive varieties, both earthly and heavenly, can disturb navigational instruments, prompting compass glitches and possibly perplexing mariners and pilots. The attractive inconsistencies inside the locale have been archived, and keeping in mind that they may not completely make sense of the range of occurrences, they add to the intricacy of exploring the Bermuda Triangle.

Methane hydrates, a type of gaseous petrol frozen under the sea depths, offer one more logical road of investigation. It is speculated that unexpected arrivals of methane gas could make lightness changes in the water, prompting the fast sinking of boats. The unstable idea of methane hydrates brings a geographical variable into the situation, proposing that the Bermuda Triangle's secrets may, to some degree, be credited to the unique powers impacting everything underneath the sea's surface.

The geographical elements of the Bermuda Triangle, for example, the remote ocean channels and submerged caves, add layers of intricacy to the area's elements. Investigating these elements is much the same as exploring through a characteristic labyrinth, where understanding the submerged scene becomes urgent to unraveling the secrets that have bewildered pilgrims for quite a long time. The sea depths, with its secret shapes and unpredictable arrangements, holds signs that coax logical examination.

Navigational difficulties inside the Bermuda Triangle, particularly during the time of early investigation, give a human aspect to the puzzle. The narratives of brave mariners wrestling with simple route apparatuses and wandering into strange waters highlight the inborn dangers of navigating this district. Understanding the verifiable setting permits us to sympathize with the sailors who, coming up short on the mechanical benefits of the current day, confronted the Bermuda Triangle as a considerable unexplored world.

Human blunder, frequently eclipsed by exciting speculations, arises as a huge calculate episodes inside the Bermuda Triangle. Examinations concerning verifiable vanishings uncover examples of confusions, navigational mix-ups, and slips by in direction. The accounts of endurance, in the midst of the conundrum, highlight the strength and versatility of people faced by the difficulties of the Bermuda Triangle. In recognizing the human component, we perceive that the secrets of the locale are not exclusively the aftereffect of outer powers but rather are laced with the unsteadiness and wins of the people who considered wandering into its waters.

Social points of view further add to the layers of the Bermuda Triangle's persona. Various societies bring their understandings, odd notions, and legends to the table, improving the account with assorted points of view. The Bermuda Triangle rises above geological limits, resounding with individuals across the globe who share an interest with the unexplored world. By embracing these social subtleties, our investigation enlarges to include a worldwide embroidery of convictions, adding lavishness to the aggregate story of the Bermuda Triangle.

Paranoid ideas, while frequently excused by standard science, have turned into a necessary piece of the Bermuda Triangle's story. Extraterrestrial inclusion, claimed government concealments, and paranormal peculiarities add to the locale's picture as a puzzling and possibly vile spot. Unraveling reality from fiction requires an insightful assessment of the impact of media emotionalism and social predispositions on the propagation of trick stories.

The Bermuda Triangle's conundrum stretches out past the limits of the geographic district. It turns into an image, a similitude for the more extensive human interest with the unexplored world. The appeal of secrets, whether established in logical abnormalities, verifiable occurrences, or social translations, spellbinds our creative mind. The Bermuda Triangle turns into a pot for investigating the outskirts of human comprehension, where the known and the obscure meet.

As we keep on making way for unwinding the conundrum, it becomes obvious that a far reaching investigation requests a blend of different points of view. The Bermuda Triangle's secrets, as opposed to capitulating to particular clarifications, flourish in the transaction of science, history, culture, and human experience. Our excursion into the core of this puzzle isn't only a mission for replies; it is an affirmation of the multifaceted snare of elements that have woven the Bermuda Triangle into the texture of our aggregate interest.

All in all, the stage set for disentangling the riddle of the Bermuda Triangle is one of intricacy, profundity, and multidimensionality. It coaxes us to move toward the secrets with a mix of logical meticulousness, verifiable setting, and social responsiveness. The Bermuda Triangle, as an image of the obscure, provokes us to rise above shortsighted clarifications and welcomes us to embrace the lavishness of its story. In our quest for disentangling the puzzle, we explore not just the geological waters of the Bermuda Triangle yet in addition the flows of human creative mind, logical request, and the immortal mission for grasping the secrets that lie into the great beyond.

Chapter 2

The Sirens' Call

The Alarms' Call: Unwinding Oceanic Old stories in the Bermuda Triangle

The Bermuda Triangle, a locale saturated with secret, has for some time been related with oceanic legends that rises above the limits among the real world and fantasy. At the core of this persona lies "The Alarms' Call," a figurative request that entices wayfarers and mariners into the profundities of the Bermuda Triangle. This part dives into the ethereal domain of sea old stories, investigating stories of spooky specters, abnormal sounds, and unexplained lights that have woven themselves into the texture of the locale's story.

The charm of The Alarms' Call exudes from the rich embroidered artwork of nautical practices that range hundreds of years. Early mariners, exploring the deceptive waters of the Atlantic, discussed experiences with supernatural peculiarities that challenged clarification. Spooky boats, enlightened by a scary shine, were said to emerge not too far off, just to disappear suddenly. These unearthly phantoms became necessary to the legend of the Bermuda Triangle, epitomizing The Alarms' Call — an enticing greeting that covered the dangers hiding underneath the surface.

The ethereal lights, frequently alluded to as apparition lights or ghost ships, are key to The Alarms' Call account. Witnesses depict glowing circles moving not too far off, enamoring the consideration of mariners and drawing them toward the unexplored world. These lights, at times confused with heavenly bodies or far off vessels, add to the persona of the Bermuda Triangle, where the conventional becomes imbued with a supernatural quality. The Alarms' Call, typified in these enamoring lights, fills in as a similitude for the compelling charm that has driven numerous to wander into the perplexing waters.

The hear-able part of The Alarms' Call presents a creepy orchestra of weird sounds that resound through the sea legends of the Bermuda Triangle. Stories proliferate of mariners hearing illogical commotions — murmurs in the breeze, tormenting tunes, or ghost cries that reverberation across the waves. These hear-able deceptions, whether results of environmental circumstances or the human creative mind, add layers of intricacy to The Alarms' Call, making a vivid encounter where the limits among the real world and the heavenly haze.

The Alarms' Call, as a story component, interlaces with the more extensive social and verifiable setting of oceanic investigation. The idea of overpowering calls attracting mariners into potential harm is profoundly imbued in different societies around the world. The legendary charm of alarms from Greek folklore, captivating mariners with their tunes and driving them to their destruction, tracks down reverberation in The Alarms' Call of the Bermuda Triangle. This paradigm fills in as a general theme, taking advantage of base feelings of trepidation and wants related with the obscure spans of the ocean.

Voyagers exploring the Bermuda Triangle during the Period of Disclosure confronted The Alarms' Call as an existential test. The shortfall of current route instruments and the dependence on heavenly direction intensified the persona of the area. Pilots, defying the vulnerability of unfamiliar waters and unusual climate, were powerless to The Alarms' Call as a mental peculiarity — one that played on their feelings of trepidation and tried their purpose to explore through the secretive triangle.

The Alarms' Call takes on a nuanced aspect as we consider the mental effect on the people who cross the Bermuda Triangle. The stories of spooky spirits and baffling lights, whether established in optical deceptions, barometrical circumstances, or the mental pressure of exploring obscure waters, add to a story where discernment and reality entwine. The Alarms' Call turns into a sign of the mental difficulties looked by mariners, welcoming us to investigate the exchange between the human psyche and the perplexing powers of the Bermuda Triangle.

In the archives of Bermuda Triangle legend, explicit episodes exemplify The Alarms' Call with specific reverberation. The Mary Celeste, a boat found uncontrolled in 1872 with its team strangely absent, brings out the frightful nature of oceanic legends. While the Mary Celeste isn't straightforwardly connected with the Bermuda Triangle, its story reflects the model of vessels viewed as deserted and brings up issues about The Alarms' Call — was it an ethereal request that drove the team to leave their boat, or were more unremarkable elements at play?

The vanishing of Flight 19 of every 1945, a group of U.S. Naval force planes, acquaints an aeronautical aspect with The Alarms' Call. The pilots, revealing compass glitches and becoming perplexed, succumbed to a figurative cancel that baited them course. The ensuing vanishing of a salvage plane, shipped off look for Flight 19, develops the story of The Alarms' Call as a mysterious power that rises above the limits among ocean and sky.

As we explore the waters of The Alarms' Call, it is fundamental to recognize the allegorical appeal of oceanic legends and the viable difficulties looked by guides in the Bermuda Triangle. The rich embroidery of legends, while suggestive, coincides with logical and navigational clarifications for the secrets related with the locale.

The interchange of fantasy and reality makes a story scene where The Alarms' Call turns into an emblematic articulation of the intrinsic dangers and vulnerabilities of oceanic investigation.

In the advanced period, The Alarms' Call continues in mainstream society through books, narratives, and fictionalized accounts. The charm of the obscure, epitomized in the spooky lights and ghost boats of sea fables, keeps on dazzling the public creative mind. The Bermuda Triangle, with its Alarms' Call, rises above its geographic limits to turn into a representation for the more extensive human interest with the secrets that sneak past the recognizable skylines.

All in all, The Alarms' Call addresses an enthralling feature of the Bermuda Triangle's persona, winding around together the strings of sea legends, verifiable stories, and social models. The allegorical request, encapsulated in spooky lights and peculiar sounds, welcomes us to investigate the mental and existential components of route in the Bermuda Triangle. As we explore through the waters of The Alarms' Call, we experience a domain where the limits among legend and reality obscure, and the puzzler of the Bermuda Triangle takes on a ghastly quality that resounds with the immortal charm of the unexplored world.

2.1 Exploring legendary tales and myths surrounding the Bermuda Triangle.

Investigating Amazing Stories and Fantasies Encompassing the Bermuda Triangle: Unwinding the Persona

The Bermuda Triangle, frequently named "Satan's Triangle," has become inseparable from a reiteration of incredible stories and fantasies that summon a feeling of secret, dread, and interest. This section leaves on an excursion into the core of these accounts, digging into the narratives that have added to the getting through persona encompassing this cryptic locale. From phantom boats to time travels, from ocean beasts to extraterrestrial experiences, the Bermuda Triangle's unbelievable stories structure a rich embroidery that rises above the limits of the real world and enters the domain of the fantastical.

Perhaps of the most persevering and chilling legend inside the Bermuda Triangle is that of the apparition transport, the Mary Celeste. While not straightforwardly connected with the actual triangle, the story of the Mary Celeste adds a phantom aspect to the district's legend. Found uncontrolled in 1872 with its freight flawless however its team strangely missing, the Mary Celeste turned into an image of sea secret. Speculations proliferate with respect to the destiny of the team, going from privateer assaults to the ocean beasts, and the legend of the Mary Celeste fills in as an eerie preamble to the horde secrets that would later be credited to the Bermuda Triangle.

In the domain of aeronautics, the vanishing of Flight 19 in December 1945 stands as one of the most notable and bewildering stories related with the Bermuda Triangle. A unit of five U.S. Naval force planes set out on a standard preparation mission and broadly evaporated suddenly. The pilots, detailing compass breakdowns and becoming confused, ultimately vanished altogether. The resulting search and salvage mission experienced its own secretive destiny, with a salvage plane likewise vanishing. The legend of Flight 19 not just denoted a significant second in the Bermuda Triangle's persona yet in addition established the groundwork for stories of airplane evaporating like a phantom, abandoning a tradition of hypothesis and marvel.

Ocean beasts, long a staple of sea fables, have tracked down a home inside the incredible stories of the Bermuda Triangle. Stories flourish of mariners experiencing titanic monsters with arms that span toward the surface, suggestive of the legendary Kraken. While such stories might be excused as results of overactive minds, the determination of ocean beast legends inside the Bermuda Triangle account adds a component of imagination and miracle to the locale's persona. These incredible animals, whether genuine or envisioned, add to the feeling that the Bermuda Triangle is where the standard principles of nature are suspended.

Extraterrestrial experiences comprise one more spellbinding element of the Bermuda Triangle's legends. The possibility that outsider powers might be answerable for the baffling vanishings and peculiarities inside the area has built up momentum in mainstream society. Speculations range from outsider kidnappings to the presence of submerged extraterrestrial bases. While lacking logical legitimacy, these extraterrestrial fantasies have become profoundly imbued in the Bermuda Triangle's account, mirroring mankind's getting through interest with the chance of powerful mediation.

Time travels and layered peculiarities address one more layer of the Bermuda Triangle's legendary scene. Stories of boats and airplane apparently evaporating from one aspect just to return in one more have powered hypothesis about the presence of entrances inside the triangle. The idea of time travels adds a sci-fi component to the locale's legends, recommending that the Bermuda Triangle might be an entryway to different domains or even various moments. These accounts, while lacking experimental proof, tap into the human creative mind's ability to imagine the phenomenal.

The legend of the USS Cyclops, a giant U.S. Naval force freight transport that vanished without a follow in 1918, contributes a verifiable aspect to the Bermuda Triangle's legends. The boat, continuing 300 team individuals and a heap of manganese mineral, was on the way from Brazil to Baltimore when it evaporated. Regardless of broad inquiry endeavors, no destruction or flotsam and jetsam was at any point found, abandoning a verifiable riddle that has become meaningful of the Bermuda Triangle's secrets. The USS Cyclops, similar to a phantom from an earlier time, torment the records of oceanic history, highlighting the locale's standing as where boats can evaporate suddenly.

The Bermuda Triangle's incredible stories frequently entwine with laid out sea and aeronautical episodes, intensifying their persona. The extravagance yacht Black magic, detailed missing off the shore of Miami in 1972 in spite of good weather patterns, adds a contemporary part to the district's fantasies. The yacht's vanishing, combined with the absence of misery signals, astounded examiners and added one more layer to the account of peculiar events inside the Bermuda Triangle. The Black magic, similar to the Mary Celeste before it, epitomizes the advanced continuation of the Bermuda Triangle's unbelievable stories.

The steadiness of these unbelievable stories brings up central issues about the human relationship with the unexplored world. Whether established in verifiable occasions, mental peculiarities, or the ripe ground of creative mind, the Bermuda Triangle's legends act as useful examples and watchfulness banners, encouraging mariners and pilots to move toward the locale with a feeling of wonderment and fear. These legends, woven into the texture of sea fables, add to a shared perspective that sees the Bermuda Triangle as a spot where reality and fantasy merge.

Mainstream society plays had a significant impact in sustaining and enhancing the unbelievable stories of the Bermuda Triangle. Books, narratives, and fictionalized accounts have changed these legends into amazing stories that enthrall crowds around the world. The Bermuda Triangle, from the perspective of mainstream society, turns into a phase where the remarkable unfurls — where the limits among truth and fiction obscure, and the legends take on a unique kind of energy.

While doubters and researchers might expose a considerable lot of the Bermuda Triangle's unbelievable stories, the getting through allure of these legends addresses a more profound human longing for secret and experience. The legends, no matter what their authentic premise, have turned into a basic piece of the Bermuda Triangle's character. They act as wake up calls, enamoring stories that rise above reality, and a demonstration of the persevering through force of the unexplored world.

All in all, the investigation of unbelievable stories and fantasies encompassing the Bermuda Triangle discloses a mind boggling embroidery of stories that have molded the locale's persona. From phantom boats to extraterrestrial experiences, from ocean beasts to time travels, the amazing stories add to the puzzler that keeps on spellbinding the human creative mind. As we explore the waters of the Bermuda Triangle's fantasies, we experience a domain where reality and dream coincide, and the unbelievable stories become a demonstration of the getting through charm of the unexplored world.

2.2 Historical context of maritime folklore influencing perceptions.

Authentic Setting of Sea Legends Affecting Insights: Exploring the Oceans of Creative mind

The sea legends encompassing the Bermuda Triangle is profoundly interwoven with the verifiable setting of nautical investigation and the difficulties looked by sailors through the ages. This part sets out on an investigation of the authentic roots that have formed the impression of the Bermuda Triangle, inspecting how hundreds of years of oceanic encounters, strange notions, and social convictions have added to the getting through persona of this confounding area.

The Time of Disclosure, a period spreading over from the late fifteenth to the mid seventeenth hundreds of years, denoted a significant period in sea investigation. European countries, driven by the longing for new shipping lanes and domains, set forth into strange waters, confronting the vulnerabilities of the vast ocean. The Bermuda Triangle, arranged amidst these Atlantic courses, turned into a considerable test for mariners exploring the deceptive waters with simple navigational devices and restricted information on the district's quirks.

During this time, the Bermuda Triangle procured a standing as a position of hazard and secret. Sailors talked about compasses acting inconsistently, unusual lights not too far off, and erratic weather conditions. The absence of exact diagrams and the presence of moving sea flows established a climate where route was a science as well as a craftsmanship — a fragile harmony between expertise, instinct, and a profound comprehension of the ocean's states of mind. These difficulties established the groundwork for the rise of oceanic legends, as mariners looked to figure out the odd peculiarities they experienced inside the triangle.

The Bermuda Triangle's authentic setting is permeated with stories of spooky ghosts and apparition delivers that spooky the fantasies of mariners exploring the Atlantic. The shortfall of substantial clarifications for vessels that disappeared without a follow led to accounts of reviled waters and malicious spirits. The Bermuda Triangle, as a geographic district, turned into a material whereupon sailors painted their feelings of dread and vulnerabilities, making a rich embroidery of sea old stories that would persevere for a really long time.

The account of apparition ships, similar to the scandalous Flying Dutchman, found reverberation inside the Bermuda Triangle's verifiable setting. Legends of vessels sentenced to cruise the oceans forever, their teams lost to the secrets of the triangle, added a ghostly quality to the locale's legend. The idea of reviled ships, everlastingly meandering the waters without rest, became significant of the difficulties looked by mariners inside the Bermuda Triangle and added to the improvement of a story where the customary principles of route appeared to unwind.

The navigational difficulties of the Bermuda Triangle during the Period of Disclosure were exacerbated by the shortfall of dependable diagrams and navigational milestones. Early guides portrayed huge unfamiliar regions, adding to the quality of the obscure that encompassed the triangle. Mariners, dependent on heavenly route and simple instruments, entered these unfamiliar waters with a feeling of fear. The absence of navigational guides changed the Bermuda Triangle into a fresh start where creative mind and odd notion could thrive, leading to stories of ocean beasts and legendary animals that hid underneath the surface.

Ocean beasts, a repetitive subject in sea legends around the world, found a home inside the Bermuda Triangle's verifiable setting. Stories of monster monsters with limbs that came to toward the surface, similar to the legendary Kraken, turned out to be important for the nautical account. While current science might excuse these accounts as embellishments or optical deceptions, the verifiable setting of the Bermuda Triangle uncovers a period when the secrets of the profound were simply starting to be perceived. Ocean beasts, whether genuine or envisioned, addressed the fearsome obscure that sailors experienced as they cruised into unknown waters.

The social setting of the Bermuda Triangle's authentic story stretches out past European oceanic practices to include the rich woven artwork of convictions and odd notions brought by different nautical networks. Social impacts from the Caribbean, with its own set of experiences of powerful old stories, mixed with European accounts to make a syncretic perspective on the Bermuda Triangle as a position of mystical authenticity. The impact of African, Native, and Caribbean societies added layers of intricacy to the district's insights, forming a story where the otherworldly and the reasonable coincided.

The infamous act of "dead retribution," a strategy for route in light of evaluations of a vessel's speed and heading, further added to the verifiable setting of the Bermuda Triangle. Pilots, lacking exact instruments, frequently depended on dead retribution to decide their situation. In the unusual waters of the triangle, where sea flows could quickly modify a boat's direction, dead retribution ended up being a shaky strategy. Blunders in route, intensified by the absence of exact diagrams, powered the discernment that the Bermuda Triangle was where navigational instruments fizzled and conventional strategies were problematic.

The presentation of the attractive compass, a significant navigational instrument, added both utility and intricacy to the verifiable setting of the Bermuda Triangle. While the compass worked with route, the district's attractive oddities made compasses act whimsically, prompting navigational difficulties. The conjunction of attractive varieties, moving sea flows, and capricious weather conditions established a climate where the Bermuda Triangle turned into a navigational riddle, testing the abilities and flexibility of sailors.

As the hundreds of years advanced, the verifiable setting of the Bermuda Triangle developed with progressions in innovation and investigation. The appearance of steamships and, later, fueled airplane didn't dispose of the difficulties related with the triangle yet rather changed them. The charm of the obscure persevered, and the Bermuda Triangle kept on being where the line between the known and the baffling stayed obscured.

The Second Great War, a time of uplifted oceanic and ethereal action, added another part to the verifiable setting of the Bermuda Triangle. The locale, currently covered in persona, turned into a point of convergence for military tasks. The vanishing of Flight 19 of every 1945, a group of U.S. Naval force planes, exemplified the difficulties of exploring the triangle even with trend setting innovation. The occurrence, with its reports of compass glitches and confusion, reverberated with verifiable stories of navigational troubles inside the Bermuda Triangle, intensifying the locale's standing as a puzzling and possibly unsafe field.

The post-war period saw an expanded interest in the secrets of the Bermuda Triangle, energized to some degree by the scattering of data through broad communications. Books, articles, and narratives added to the promotion of the locale's verifiable setting, acquainting a worldwide crowd with the stories of vanishings, bizarre events, and oceanic fables. The Bermuda Triangle, when a navigational test for mariners, changed into a social peculiarity that rose above its topographical limits.

In the last 50% of the twentieth 100 years, logical request looked to disentangle the secrets of the Bermuda Triangle. Oceanography, meteorology, and geophysics gave clarifications to a portion of the peculiarities related with the district. The Inlet Stream, a strong sea momentum coursing through the triangle, was distinguished as a supporter of violent oceans and eccentric climate. Attractive abnormalities, brought about by varieties in the World's attractive field, were pinpointed as variables influencing navigational instruments. While these logical clarifications tended to certain parts of the Bermuda Triangle's secrets, they didn't completely scatter the verifiable setting of sea fables that had become profoundly imbued in the district's personality.

Verifiable Setting of Sea Legends Impacting Insights: Exploring the Oceans of Creative mind

As we dig further into the authentic setting of sea fables encompassing the Bermuda Triangle, it becomes obvious that the exchange among reality and fiction has profound roots in the human experience of exploring the oceans. The diverse idea of this setting incorporates the difficulties looked by mariners as well as the advancing innovations, social impacts, and worldwide interest that have molded the Bermuda Triangle's riddle.

The Time of Sail, a period that traversed the sixteenth to the mid-nineteenth hundreds of years, assumed a critical part in forming the verifiable setting of the Bermuda Triangle. During this time, cruising vessels turned into the essential method for significant distance transportation and investigation. The three-sided shipping lanes, associating Europe, Africa, and the Americas, crossed with the Bermuda Triangle, presenting mariners to the area's difficulties. The supposed "Villain's Ocean," as it was in some cases known, turned into a cauldron for the improvement of sea fables as mariners wrestled with the vulnerabilities of the vast sea.

Without a trace of current navigational instruments, early sailors depended intensely on divine route and the stars to direct their vessels. The night sky, with its groups of stars and astral designs, turned into a divine guide for mariners. Nonetheless, the Bermuda Triangle's infamous standing for unpredictable compass conduct and claimed attractive inconsistencies added a layer of intricacy to this generally difficult route. The heavenly bodies that directed mariners took on an extra importance inside the verifiable setting of the Bermuda Triangle, as sailors looked for comfort and bearing from the stars in the midst of the secrets of the area.

The verifiable story of the Bermuda Triangle is additionally accentuated by records of baffling lights not too far off, adding to the locale's quality of persona. Early mariners, coming up short on the logical comprehension of environmental peculiarities, would have deciphered these lights as powerful or extraordinary. The

St. Elmo's Fire peculiarity, brought about by the ionization of air particles, may make sense of a portion of these sightings, yet inside the verifiable setting, they became reference points of the obscure, supporting the Bermuda Triangle's standing as where reality and odd notion interweaved.

The advancement of navigational devices, especially the attractive compass, further characterizes the verifiable setting of the Bermuda Triangle. While the compass altered route, it likewise presented a component of weakness. The Bermuda Triangle's attractive oddities, where the World's attractive field acts unpredictably, could prompt compass deviations, making disarray for mariners who depended on this key instrument. The strain between the commitment of innovative progression and the difficulties presented by the locale's one of a kind attractive qualities formed the story of the Bermuda Triangle as a spot where even the most complex instruments could flounder.

The Period of Sail slowly gave way to the Time of Steam, denoting a huge change in oceanic innovation during the nineteenth 100 years. Steam-fueled ships, moved by motors as opposed to wind, guaranteed more noteworthy control and dependability in route. Be that as it may, the Bermuda Triangle's authentic setting persevered, adjusting to the evolving times. Steamships, while offering new abilities, were not resistant to the difficulties presented by the locale's unusual flows and unfriendly weather patterns. The change from sail to steam didn't scatter the oceanic fables; all things considered, it developed to envelop the subtleties of another time.

The coming of steam power additionally corresponded with a time of expanded logical request and understanding. Meteorology, the investigation of weather conditions, started to give clarifications to the abrupt and rough tempests revealed inside the Bermuda Triangle. While logical headways intended to demystify a portion of the locale's peculiarities, the instilled verifiable setting of oceanic fables continued, making a polarity between normal clarifications and the getting through charm of the unexplored world.

The social impacts inside the verifiable setting of the Bermuda Triangle are assorted and envelop an embroidery woven from the convictions of various marine networks. The Caribbean, with its rich history of voodoo and heavenly customs, added a layer of otherworldliness to the district. The combination of African, Native, and European social impacts inside the Caribbean added to the improvement of a special story encompassing the Bermuda Triangle — one that embraced the magical and the functional in equivalent measure.

Social convictions in spirits, ocean beasts, and charmed waters tracked down reverberation inside the authentic setting, molding discernments and adding to the getting through fables of the Bermuda Triangle. Mariners from different social foundations carried their notions and customs to the ocean, looking for assurance from the obscure powers that snuck inside the triangle. The combination of these different social components made a story that rose above topographical limits, laying out the Bermuda Triangle as a spot where the heavenly existed together with the ordinary.

The worldwide interest with the obscure, filled by investigation and sea takes advantage of, further formed the authentic setting of the Bermuda Triangle. As reports of puzzling vanishings and unexplained peculiarities flowed through papers and periodicals, the area caught the creative mind of the public around the world. The Bermuda Triangle turned into an image of the mysterious and the unsafe — where the secrets of the ocean appeared in manners that resisted ordinary clarification.

The coming of the message and later, the broad communications during the twentieth hundred years, assumed a significant part in spreading stories and molding view of the Bermuda Triangle. Reports of vanishings, bizarre events, and asserted otherworldly peculiarities contacted crowds internationally, enhancing the district's standing. The line among reality and fiction obscured as sensationalized stories added to the development of the Bermuda Triangle as a social peculiarity.

The Second Great War, a time of extreme maritime and elevated action, infused another aspect into the verifiable setting of the Bermuda Triangle. The locale turned into a vital point of convergence for military tasks, and the difficulties looked by pilots and guides additionally filled the persona of the triangle. The vanishing of Flight 19, a unit of U.S. Naval force planes, turned into an extremely important occasion that repeated the verifiable battles of sailors inside the Bermuda Triangle. The wartime setting added a layer of desperation and interest to the story, hardening the locale's status as a confounding and possibly risky region.

The post-war time saw a flood in broad daylight interest, prodded by headways in flying, oceanography, and logical investigation. Specialists looked to disentangle the secrets of the Bermuda Triangle, applying a logical focal point to peculiarities that had for some time been covered in legend. While clarifications arose for a portion of the vanishings credited to the Bermuda Triangle, the verifiable setting of sea old stories endured, opposing total digestion into the domain of logical comprehension.

In the last option part of the twentieth 100 years, the Bermuda Triangle rose above its geographic limits to turn into a social symbol. Books, narratives, and movies propagated the verifiable setting of oceanic old stories, depicting the district as a position of mysterious secrets and otherworldly powers. The Bermuda Triangle, when a navigational test for mariners, changed into an image that caught the worldwide creative mind — an image that repeated the verifiable battles, social impacts, and innovative progressions that molded its mysterious story.

As we explore the oceans of creative mind inside the verifiable setting of the Bermuda Triangle, it becomes obvious that this locale is in excess of a geographic oddity; it is a juncture of verifiable encounters, social convictions, and human interest with the unexplored world. The exchange between oceanic old stories and the developing story of the Bermuda Triangle highlights the intricacy of human insight, helping us that the secrets to remember the ocean are as much a result of creative mind as they are of logical request. In this proceeded with investigation, we explore the waters of the Bermuda Triangle as well as the flows of mankind's set of experiences, culture, and the persevering through charm of the puzzling oceans.

All in all, the verifiable setting of sea legends plays had a vital impact in forming impression of the Bermuda Triangle. From the difficulties looked by voyagers during the Period of Disclosure to the impact of social convictions and strange notions, the account of the Bermuda Triangle mirrors the mind boggling exchange between authentic encounters and the human creative mind. The locale's standing as a position of secret, energized by hundreds of years of marine legend, keeps on spellbinding the shared perspective. As we explore the oceans of creative mind inside the verifiable setting of the Bermuda Triangle, we experience a domain where the known and the obscure combine, making an embroidery of sea fables that perseveres through the ages.

Chapter 3

Vanishing Acts

Evaporating Acts: Unwinding the Secrets of Vanishings in the Bermuda Triangle

The Bermuda Triangle, notorious for its indicated secretive vanishings of boats and airplane, has become inseparable from the idea of disappearing acts. This part digs into the puzzler of evaporating acts inside the Bermuda Triangle, investigating verifiable occurrences, telling stories of astounding vanishings, and analyzing the different speculations that endeavor to disentangle this persevering through secret.

One of the earliest and most notorious evaporating acts related with the Bermuda Triangle traces all the way back to the nineteenth 100 years — the vanishing of the USS Cyclops in 1918. This huge U.S. Naval force freight transport, with a team of more than 300 and a heap of manganese mineral, disappeared without a follow while in transit from Brazil to Baltimore. In spite of broad hunt endeavors, no destruction or trash was at any point found. The USS Cyclops became symbolic of the Bermuda Triangle's secrets, a vessel gulped by the mysterious waters without abandoning a solitary sign. The occurrence highlighted the difficulties looked by guides in the district and set up for a progression of disappearing acts that would catch the public's creative mind.

Flight 19, a unit of five U.S. Naval force aircraft, is maybe the most eminent disappearing act inside the Bermuda Triangle. In December 1945, during a normal preparation mission, Flight 19 vanished suddenly. The pilots, revealing compass breakdowns and becoming confused, in the long run ran out of fuel and needed to discard adrift. The resulting search and salvage mission, known as Flight 19's "Lost Watch," experienced its own evaporating go about as the salvage plane likewise vanished suddenly. The baffling vanishing of Flight 19 and its future heros filled hypothesis about the Bermuda Triangle's capacity to eradicate both airplane and those shipped off track down them — a disrupting demonstration of the district's getting through persona.

"

The appeal of evaporating acts reaches out past military activities to regular citizen vessels, exemplified by the Mary Celeste — a scandalous phantom boat that catches the quintessence of oceanic secrets. While the Mary Celeste isn't straightforwardly connected with the Bermuda Triangle, its story adds a ghastly aspect to the idea of evaporating follows up on the vast ocean. Found hapless in 1872 with its freight flawless yet its team bafflingly missing, the Mary Celeste turned into an image of sea puzzle, a vessel deserted without evident reason. However not inside the geographic limits of the Bermuda Triangle, the Mary Celeste's story repeats the more extensive subject of unexplained vanishings that has become inseparable from the area.

In the domain of avionics, the disappearing acts inside the Bermuda Triangle have reached out to business flights, further enhancing the secret. The instance of Flight 441 out of 1948 embodies this pattern. A Douglas DC-3 airplanes, in transit from San Juan, Puerto Rico, to Miami, vanished without a misery call or any difficult situation. In spite of broad pursuit endeavors, no destruction or flotsam and jetsam was at any point found. The evaporating demonstration of Flight 441 added to the developing inventory of strange aeronautics secrets inside the Bermuda Triangle, leaving examiners and the general population baffled.

The Black magic, a cutting edge extravagance yacht, added to the story of evaporating acts in the Bermuda Triangle. In 1967, the Black magic vanished off the shoreline of Miami under apparently great weather patterns. Regardless of the yacht's high level route gear and the vicinity to shore, no trouble signals were gotten, and no destruction was found. The evaporating demonstration of the Black magic, combined with the absence of an obvious reason, added a contemporary section to the Bermuda Triangle's mystery, testing the overall faith in mechanical progressions relieving the dangers related with the district.

The idea of evaporating acts inside the Bermuda Triangle isn't bound to vessels alone; it reaches out to airplane of different sizes and types. One such occurrence included a Martin Sailor flying boat in 1954. During a normal preparation mission, the airplane, conveying 13 group individuals, vanished suddenly. Regardless of broad hunt endeavors, no destruction or trash was found. The evaporating demonstration of the Martin Sailor added to the developing rundown of airplane bafflingly lost inside the Bermuda Triangle, adding to the locale's standing as where the common principles of route appeared to unwind.

Hypotheses endeavoring to make sense of the disappearing acts inside the Bermuda Triangle are just about as shifted as the actual episodes. Attractive irregularities, which can influence navigational instruments, are many times refered to as expected guilty parties. The Bermuda Triangle is known for its attractive varieties, and a few scholars recommend that these oddities could prompt compass breakdowns, confusing pilots and mariners and adding to their vanishing. While attractive oddities are an unmistakable part of the locale, their immediate connection with evaporating acts stays a subject of discussion inside established researchers.

Another hypothesis recommends that submerged elements, for example, remote ocean channels or submerged volcanoes, could be answerable for the disappearing acts inside the Bermuda Triangle. As indicated by this hypothesis, boats and airplane could experience these highlights startlingly, prompting disastrous occasions and vanishings. While the sea depths in the Bermuda Triangle includes some remote ocean channels and land structures, the degree to which they add to disappearing acts stays speculative and needs decisive proof.

The Bay Stream, a strong sea momentum moving through the Bermuda Triangle, has likewise been ensnared in speculations making sense of disappearing acts. The quick and tempestuous nature of the Inlet Stream could prompt the fast vanishing of destruction, making it trying for search and salvage groups to find trash. Also, the Bay Stream's effect on weather conditions might add to abrupt and savage tempests that could overpower vessels and airplane. While the Bay Stream is a perceived figure the district's elements, its part in the evaporating acts stays a mind boggling puzzle with numerous factors.

A few hypotheses drift into the domain of sci-fi, proposing the presence of sub-merged extraterrestrial bases or time travels inside the Bermuda Triangle. These speculative thoughts recommend that outsider powers or fleeting abnormalities could be liable for the unexplained vanishings. While these speculations catch the creative mind and find a spot in mainstream society, they need observational proof and logical help.

The evaporating acts inside the Bermuda Triangle have started banters among cynics and advocates of paranormal clarifications. Cynics contend that numerous occurrences can be ascribed to normal peculiarities, human mistake, or navigational difficulties, and that the Bermuda Triangle's standing is expanded by specific de-tailing and emotionalism. Defenders of paranormal clarifications, then again, fight that the sheer volume of unexplained vanishings inside the locale recommends the presence of exceptional and perhaps extraordinary powers.

Notwithstanding these hypotheses and discussions, it is fundamental to recog-nize that the Bermuda Triangle's disappearing acts exist inside a more extensive setting of sea and aeronautical difficulties. The locale is inclined to unusual weather conditions, quick flows, and navigational challenges, all of which can add to oceanic and flying episodes. The disappearing acts, while puzzling and spellbinding, should be viewed as inside the structure of the innate dangers related with exploring mind boggling and dynamic conditions.

The getting through interest with the disappearing acts inside the Bermuda Triangle stretches out past the domain of logical request. Mainstream society, filled by books, narratives, and fictionalized accounts, has propagated the persona of the locale's vanishings. The Bermuda Triangle has turned into an image of the obscure and the unexplained, catching the public creative mind and adding to a social story where the common changes into the phenomenal.

All in all, the evaporating acts inside the Bermuda Triangle comprise a dazzling and getting through secret that rises above the limits of geology and time. From verifiable maritime vessels to current airplane and extravagance yachts, the conundrum of vanishings endures, testing how we might interpret the oceans and skies. As we explore the waters of hypothesis and logical request, the disappearing acts inside the Bermuda Triangle stay a demonstration of the intricacy of the normal world and the human limit with respect to ponder notwithstanding the unexplored world.

3.1 In-depth examination of famous disappearances.

Top to bottom Assessment of Renowned Vanishings in the Bermuda Triangle: Disentangling the Woven artwork of Secret

The Bermuda Triangle, a locale notorious for its indicated strange vanishings of boats and airplane, has woven an embroidery of conundrum that stretches across many years. This section sets out on a top to bottom assessment of probably the most popular vanishings inside the Bermuda Triangle, digging into the subtleties of these occurrences, investigating the predominant hypotheses, and trying to unwind the intricacies that encompass every vanishing.

Quite possibly of the most persevering and strange vanishing inside the Bermuda Triangle is that of Flight 19 in December 1945. This unit of five U.S. Naval force planes, drove by experienced flight teacher Lieutenant Charles Taylor, set out on a normal preparation mission from the Maritime Air Station in Post Lauderdale, Florida. Be that as it may, what happened during the mission would turn into the stuff of legend. The pilots revealed compass breakdowns, professed to be perplexed, and in the end radioed that they couldn't decide their area. As fuel ran short, Flight 19 vanished suddenly. The ensuing inquiry and salvage mission, known as Flight 19's "Lost Watch," experienced its own evaporating go about as a salvage plane likewise vanished suddenly. The strange vanishing of Flight 19 remaining parts one of the most notorious and confounding stories related with the Bermuda Triangle.

The Mary Celeste, however not straightforwardly inside the geological limits of the Bermuda Triangle, is a phantom boat that adds an unpleasant aspect to the locale's puzzle. Found hapless in the Atlantic in 1872, the Mary Celeste was without its group, who appeared to have evaporated suddenly. The boat's freight, including significant liquor, was immaculate, and there were no indications of battle or misery. The secretive conditions encompassing the Mary Celeste have filled hypothesis and guess for north of a really long period. While the genuine reason for the group's vanishing stays obscure, the Mary Celeste is in many cases conjured as a model of sea secret, repeating the topics related with the Bermuda Triangle.

In the domain of military flying, the vanishing of Flight 441 out of 1948 added one more layer to the Bermuda Triangle's persona. This Douglas DC-3 airplanes, worked by the U.S. Aviation based armed forces, was in transit from San Juan, Puerto Rico, to Miami. Notwithstanding clear weather patterns and the dependability of the airplane, Flight 441 vanished without a pain call or any difficult situation. The quest for destruction demonstrated vain, and the airplane appeared to have evaporated suddenly. The disappearing demonstration of Flight 441, as so many others, added to the feeling of unusualness and vulnerability that portrays the Bermuda Triangle.

The Black magic, an extravagance yacht, acquainted a cutting edge part with the Bermuda Triangle's inventory of vanishings. In 1967, the Black magic set out from Miami on a twilight night for a short journey. In spite of being just a mile seaward and outfitted with the most recent navigational innovation, the yacht strangely vanished. The absence of misery signals, great atmospheric conditions, and the vicinity to the coast puzzled specialists. The evaporating demonstration of the Black magic tested the thought that mechanical progressions had alleviated the dangers related with the Bermuda Triangle, featuring that even in the period of refined route, the secrets persevered.

The Martin Sailor flying boat occurrence in 1954 embodies the scope of airplane engaged with the Bermuda Triangle's vanishings. During a normal preparation mission, this huge airplane, with a wingspan comparable to that of a Boeing 747, vanished suddenly. The airplane was conveying 13 group individuals, and in spite of broad pursuit endeavors, no destruction or trash was at any point found. The evaporating demonstration of the Martin Sailor highlighted the aimless idea of the Bermuda Triangle's secrets, influencing military airplane as well as business flights and confidential vessels.

The USS Cyclops, a titanic U.S. Naval force freight transport, remains as quite possibly of the main maritime vanishing inside the Bermuda Triangle. In 1918, during The Second Great War, the USS Cyclops disappeared without a follow while on the way from Brazil to Baltimore. The boat, conveying a heap of manganese metal and more than 300 team individuals, never arrived at its objective. In spite of broad hunt endeavors, no destruction or trash was at any point found. The vanishing of the USS Cyclops stays one of the best oceanic secrets of the twentieth 100 years, adding to the Bermuda Triangle's standing as where boats can disappear without leaving a solitary hint.

The Bay Stream, a strong sea momentum moving through the Bermuda Triangle, has been ensnared in different vanishings. Its quick and fierce nature could add to the fast vanishing of destruction, making it trying for search and salvage groups to find trash. Also, the Bay Stream's effect on atmospheric conditions might prompt unexpected and rough tempests that could overpower vessels and airplane. The Bay Stream's part in vanishings adds a layer of intricacy to the Bermuda Triangle's secrets, entwining maritime elements with the stories of evaporated ships and planes.

Hypotheses endeavoring to make sense of these renowned vanishings inside the Bermuda Triangle are all around as different as the actual episodes. One common hypothesis includes attractive abnormalities, proposing that the locale's attractive varieties could prompt compass glitches, perplexing pilots and mariners. The thought is that these abnormalities could add to navigational difficulties, making vessels and airplane get sidetracked and evaporate. While attractive irregularities are a perceived component of the Bermuda Triangle, their immediate association with vanishings stays a subject of continuous discussion.

The submerged geography of the Bermuda Triangle, including remote ocean channels and submerged volcanoes, has been proposed as a likely clarification for evaporating acts. As per this hypothesis, vessels and airplane could experience these highlights suddenly, prompting disastrous occasions and vanishings. The geographical elements underneath the sea's surface are complicated, and keeping in mind that they might add to navigational difficulties, the degree to which they straightforwardly cause vanishings stays speculative.

The Bay Stream's part in vanishings is another hypothesis that lines up with the area's maritime elements. The quick and fierce nature of the current, joined with its capability to create abrupt tempests, could overpower vessels and airplane. The Bay Stream hypothesis recommends that the vanishing of destruction in the tempestuous waters might add to the trouble of finding trash during search and salvage activities. While the Bay Stream is a perceived consider the district's elements, its immediate connection with disappearing acts stays a complicated riddle with numerous factors.

A few hypotheses dig into the domain of sci-fi, proposing the presence of submerged extraterrestrial bases or time travels inside the Bermuda Triangle. These speculative thoughts recommend that outsider powers or worldly inconsistencies could be liable for the unexplained vanishings. While these hypotheses catch the creative mind and find a spot in mainstream society, they need observational proof and logical help.

Cynics contend that numerous occurrences inside the Bermuda Triangle can be ascribed to normal peculiarities, human blunder, or navigational difficulties, and that the district's standing is expanded by specific announcing and drama. Advocates of paranormal clarifications, then again, fight that the sheer volume of unexplained vanishings inside the area recommends the presence of remarkable and potentially powerful powers.

In analyzing these well known vanishings inside the Bermuda Triangle, it becomes clear that the secrets persevere in spite of many years of hypothesis, examination, and logical request. The intricacy of the vanishings, including vessels and airplane of different sizes and capacities, challenges oversimplified clarifications. The Bermuda Triangle stays a district where the known and the obscure combine, where the standard becomes phenomenal, and where the embroidery of secret keeps on unfurling.

The persevering through interest with these vanishings stretches out past logical request. Mainstream society, filled by books, narratives, and fictionalized accounts, has propagated the persona of the locale's vanishings. The Bermuda Triangle has turned into an image of the obscure and the unexplained, catching the public creative mind and adding to a social story where reality and secret blend.

All in all, the top to bottom assessment of popular vanishings inside the Bermuda Triangle uncovers a scene of interest and vulnerability. From Flight 19's "Lost Watch" to the evaporating demonstration of the USS Cyclops, every occurrence adds to the district's conundrum. Hypotheses endeavoring to make sense of these vanishings give looks into the intricacies of the Bermuda Triangle's elements, yet the real essence of the secrets stays slippery. As we explore the oceans of hypothesis and logical request, the renowned vanishings inside the Bermuda Triangle persevere as waypoints on an excursion into the obscure — an excursion where the limits among the real world and legend obscure, and the secrets of the ocean keep on enamoring the human creative mind.

3.2 Analyzing patterns and commonalities in missing ships and aircraft.

Breaking down Examples and Shared characteristics in Missing Boats and Airplane: Disentangling the Puzzler of the Bermuda Triangle

The Bermuda Triangle, a district in the western piece of the North Atlantic Sea, has procured reputation for its implied secretive vanishings of boats and airplane. Examining examples and shared characteristics in these missing vessels and planes turns into a significant endeavor in disentangling the conundrum that covers this geographic region. This section dives into a far reaching assessment of the verifiable examples, shared qualities, and repeating subjects related with the missing boats and airplane inside the Bermuda Triangle.

One eminent example that arises while examining the vanishings in the Bermuda Triangle is the eccentricism of the episodes. The vanishings don't stick to a reliable situation or variables, making it trying to pinpoint a particular reason.

Vessels and airplane of differing sizes, from little boats to huge military planes, have all accomplished unexplained vanishings inside the locale. This absence of consistency adds to the persevering through secret of the Bermuda Triangle and highlights the intricacy of breaking down the examples related with these vanishings.

One more shared characteristic among missing boats and airplane inside the Bermuda Triangle is the shortfall of misery signals or calls for help. As a rule, vessels and planes disappeared with next to no advance notice, abandoning a void of data for specialists. The unexpected and unexplained nature of these vanishings has energized hypothesis and added to the view of the Bermuda Triangle as a spot where typical correspondence channels separate. This common trademark adds a layer of interest to the examination, as the shortfall of pain signals difficulties ordinary clarifications for sea and flight occurrences.

Navigational difficulties and bizarre compass readings comprise a repetitive topic in the vanishings inside the Bermuda Triangle. Many reports from pilots and mariners portray compasses acting whimsically, with needles turning or pointing in erratic headings. This peculiarity, frequently credited to attractive oddities in the locale, acquaints an unmistakable component with the examination. The Bermuda Triangle's attractive varieties, where the World's attractive field acts conflictingly, are viewed as by some as expected supporters of navigational hardships. Be that as it may, while attractive oddities are a perceived component of the locale, the degree to which they straightforwardly cause vanishings stays a subject of progressing banter inside established researchers.

The Bay Stream, a strong sea momentum coursing through the Bermuda Triangle, arises as a huge consider the examination of missing boats and airplane. The quick and tempestuous nature of the Bay Stream can make testing conditions for vessels and add to the trouble of finding destruction. Moreover, the Inlet Stream's effect on atmospheric conditions might prompt the development of unexpected and brutal tempests, further entangling sea and avionics exercises. The predominance of vanishings in nearness to the Bay Stream brings up issues about its part in molding the examples inside the Bermuda Triangle. Dissecting verifiable climate information, oceanographic conditions, and the directions of missing vessels and planes gives an all encompassing perspective on how the Bay Stream interweaves with the puzzle of the Bermuda Triangle.

The immeasurability of the Bermuda Triangle's sea field, combined with its vicinity to vigorously dealt ocean courses, adds to the variety of vessels that have disappeared. Freight ships, military vessels, fishing boats, and delight creates have all accomplished unexplained vanishings inside the district. This variety challenges the idea that a particular sort of vessel or a particular situation is liable for the vanishings. All things being equal, the Bermuda Triangle's examples recommend a more nuanced interaction of variables that rise above the differentiations between different sorts of vessels.

Looking at the verifiable setting of missing boats inside the Bermuda Triangle uncovers an embroidery of oceanic old stories that impacts insights. Stories of spooky nebulous visions, apparition delivers, and reviled waters have saturated the locale's account, adding to the persona that encompasses it. These social impacts, established in hundreds of years of nautical practices and convictions, add a layer of intricacy to the examination. The transaction between verifiable encounters, social convictions, and the human creative mind turns into a pivotal part of understanding the examples related with missing boats in the Bermuda Triangle.

In the domain of flight, examining examples of missing airplane inside the Bermuda Triangle uncovers a particular arrangement of difficulties and shared traits. Flight vanishings frequently include experienced pilots directing routine flights, as exemplified by the renowned instance of Flight 19. The group of U.S. Naval force planes, drove by Lieutenant Charles Taylor, left on a normal preparation mission in 1945, just to vanish suddenly. This example of experienced pilots participated in recognizable exercises brings up issues about the effect of routine missions and the degree of readiness for unforeseen difficulties inside the Bermuda Triangle.

A common trademark among missing airplane is the absence of definitive proof or destruction. Regardless of broad pursuit endeavors in the consequence of vanishings, numerous airplane have never been found, abandoning a void of actual proof. This shortfall of destruction adds to the persevering through secret of the

Bermuda Triangle, as it challenges customary assumptions about the result of flight occurrences. Hypotheses about fast plunges, submerged submersion, or crumbling without leaving flotsam and jetsam stay speculative, featuring the requirement for a more exhaustive comprehension of the examples related with missing airplane.

Like the sea setting, navigational difficulties and compass peculiarities are repetitive subjects in the vanishing of airplane inside the Bermuda Triangle. Pilots have announced compass breakdowns, bewilderment, and whimsical instrument readings, reflecting the encounters of mariners in the locale. The assembly of these navigational difficulties in both sea and flying settings brings up issues about the hidden elements that add to the breakdown of navigational frameworks inside the Bermuda Triangle.

In investigating the examples and shared traits of missing boats and airplane inside the Bermuda Triangle, it becomes clear that the puzzler reaches out past short-sighted clarifications. The district's standing as a hotbed of strange vanishings is based on a complicated interaction of variables, including navigational difficulties, flighty weather patterns, and social impacts. Breaking down these examples requires a multidisciplinary approach that thinks about oceanography, meteorology, geophysics, and social humanities.

Mainstream researchers has looked to unwind the secrets of the Bermuda Triangle through experimental examinations and mechanical progressions. Oceanographic studies have revealed insight into the mind boggling flows and submerged highlights that describe the area. Meteorological examination has given bits of knowledge into the weather conditions that might add to abrupt tempests and tempestuous circumstances. Geophysical examinations have investigated the attractive abnormalities that influence navigational instruments. Notwithstanding, the test lies in coordinating these different fields of review to shape a far reaching comprehension of the examples inside the Bermuda Triangle.

As innovation keeps on propelling, apparatuses like satellite symbolism, high level sonar frameworks, and further developed navigational instruments offer new open doors for exploring the examples related with missing boats and airplane. Remote detecting innovations consider the precise checking of the district's maritime and barometrical circumstances, giving continuous information that can add to a more nuanced investigation of the Bermuda Triangle's elements. Also, progresses in submerged investigation advancements empower scientists to dive into the profundities of the sea, possibly revealing destruction or proof that has evaded disclosure before.

The social element of the Bermuda Triangle's puzzle adds a layer of intricacy to the examination of examples and shared traits. Fables, legends, and stories went down through ages impact view of the district and add to the getting through interest with its secrets. Coordinating social human sciences into the insightful structure considers a more all encompassing comprehension of how convictions, odd notions, and verifiable encounters shape the examples related with missing boats and airplane. The intermingling of logical request and social investigation is fundamental for disentangling the complex idea of the Bermuda Triangle's puzzle.

Dissecting Examples and Shared traits in Missing Boats and Airplane: A More profound Investigate the Bermuda Triangle Mystery

The Bermuda Triangle, a district infamous for its implied strange vanishings, has long enamored the creative mind of lovers and researchers the same. To grasp the examples and shared characteristics related with missing boats and airplane inside this cryptic triangle, an exhaustive assessment becomes foremost. The stories of disappeared vessels, be they maritime boats or regular citizen airplane, uncover fascinating examples that challenge direct clarifications.

One striking component is the evident irregularity of these vanishings. Dissimilar to different peculiarities with perceivable examples, the Bermuda Triangle's vanishings happen without a reliable situation. A scope of vessels — from little fishing boats to titanic freight ships — and airplane, spreading over military planes to business jets, have all capitulated to the secrets of this locale. This absence of consistency highlights the complicated idea of the Bermuda Triangle's elements, moving specialists to recognize a solitary reason.

Adding to the persona is the shortfall of pain signals or calls for help generally speaking. Vessels and planes appear to evaporate suddenly, abandoning a void of data that entangles endeavors to comprehend the occasions prompting their vanishing. This common trademark presents a component of abruptness and capriciousness, supporting the thought that the Bermuda Triangle is where typical correspondence channels separate, adding to its confounding air.

Navigational difficulties and strange compass readings arise as repeating subjects in the missing boats and airplane inside the Bermuda Triangle. Various reports portray compasses acting whimsically, with needles turning or pointing in flighty headings. This peculiarity, credited to attractive oddities in the locale, adds an unmistakable viewpoint to the examination. The Bermuda Triangle's attractive varieties, where the World's attractive field acts conflictingly, are viewed as by some as expected supporters of navigational hardships. However, in spite of their acknowledgment as an element of the district, the immediate association between attractive peculiarities and vanishings stays a subject of progressing banter.

The Bay Stream, a strong sea momentum moving through the Bermuda Triangle, arises as a huge figure the examination of missing vessels and planes. The quick and violent nature of the Bay Stream makes testing conditions for sea exercises, possibly adding to the trouble of finding destruction. Also, the Bay Stream's impact on atmospheric conditions might prompt the arrangement of abrupt and vicious tempests, further confounding both sea and avionics attempts. The commonness of vanishings in nearness to the Bay Stream brings up issues about its part in molding the examples inside the Bermuda Triangle, featuring the requirement for a nuanced comprehension of its maritime elements.

Variety is an outstanding trademark while looking at missing boats inside the

Bermuda Triangle. The area's immense oceanic scope, combined with its vicinity to intensely dealt ocean courses, adds to the variety of vessels that have evaporated. Freight ships, military vessels, fishing boats, and joy creates have all accomplished unexplained vanishings inside the locale. This variety challenges that a particular kind of vessel or a particular situation is liable for the vanishings. All things being equal, the Bermuda Triangle's examples recommend a more nuanced exchange of variables that rise above the qualifications between different sorts of vessels.

In the domain of flying, the examples related with missing airplane inside the Bermuda Triangle uncover an unmistakable arrangement of difficulties and shared traits. Experienced pilots leading routine flights frequently wind up entrapped in the secrets of the Bermuda Triangle, as found in the well known instance of Flight 19 out of 1945. The unit of U.S. Naval force planes, drove by Lieutenant Charles Taylor, set out on a normal preparation mission just to vanish suddenly. This example of experienced pilots participated in recognizable exercises brings up issues about the effect of routine missions and the degree of readiness for surprising difficulties inside the Bermuda Triangle.

A common trademark among missing airplane is the absence of indisputable proof or destruction. In spite of broad hunt endeavors, numerous airplane have never been found, abandoning a void of actual proof. This shortfall of destruction adds to the persevering through secret of the Bermuda Triangle, testing traditional assumptions about the outcome of avionics episodes.

All in all, dissecting examples and shared traits in missing boats and airplane inside the Bermuda Triangle requires a multi-faceted methodology that traverses logical disciplines and social settings. The locale's secrets, established in hundreds of years of nautical practices and propagated by current stories, request a complete comprehension that goes past oversimplified clarifications. As we explore the mind boggling flows of oceanography, meteorology, geophysics, and social human sciences, the examples inside the Bermuda Triangle stay slippery, provoking us to unwind the embroidery of secret that covers this baffling region.

Chapter 4

The Scientific Lens

The Logical Focal point: Disentangling the Mystery of the Bermuda Triangle

The Bermuda Triangle, frequently alluded to as Satan's Triangle, has for quite some time been a subject of interest and hypothesis because of its indicated secretive vanishings of boats and airplane. While the district, limited by focuses in Miami, Bermuda, and Puerto Rico, has been saturated with legends and fables, mainstream researchers has tried to see the peculiarities through an objective and proof based focal point. This investigation through the logical focal point includes analyzing different components — oceanography, meteorology, geophysics, and navigational difficulties — to demystify the baffling events inside the Bermuda Triangle.

Oceanography, the investigation of the physical and organic properties of the sea, assumes a urgent part in grasping the secrets of the Bermuda Triangle. The district is known for its mind boggling ebbs and flows, with the Bay Stream being a key part. This strong sea momentum moves through the triangle, making dynamic and at times violent circumstances.

Logical examination concerning the Bay Stream's effect on sea exercises has uncovered that the quick and unusual nature of this flow could add to the challenges looked by ships exploring through the area. The combination of numerous flows in the Bermuda Triangle makes an unpredictable snare of submerged elements, testing even the most prepared sailors.

Notwithstanding sea flows, the submerged geology of the Bermuda Triangle is set apart by remote ocean channels and submerged highlights. These geographical arrangements have been proposed as expected supporters of the strange vanishings. The thought is that vessels and airplane might experience these elements out of the blue, prompting horrendous occasions and vanishings. Logical investigation of the ocean bottom has to be sure recognized critical varieties inside and out and submerged structures, however connecting these elements straightforwardly to vanishings stays an intricate riddle. While the sea's profundities hide a lot, headways in submerged planning innovations offer promising roads for acquiring further bits of knowledge into the locale's geology.

Meteorology, the investigation of the climate and its peculiarities, gives one more layer to the logical assessment of the Bermuda Triangle. Abrupt and vicious tempests are pervasive in the district, filled to some degree by the union of exchange winds. The quick changes in weather conditions, frequently exacerbated by the Bay Stream, can make testing conditions for both sea and flight exercises. Logical examination of verifiable climate information inside the Bermuda Triangle has featured the event of rebel waves and waterspouts — peculiarities that can present huge dangers to vessels. Understanding the meteorological variables at play adds to a more far reaching evaluation of the dangers looked by boats and airplane in the district.

The Bermuda Triangle is known for its attractive inconsistencies, a variable inside the domain of geophysics. The World's attractive field encounters abnormalities in the district, prompting compass varieties that have been refered to in many reports of navigational difficulties. Logical examinations concerning attractive peculiarities inside the Bermuda Triangle have looked to comprehend what these varieties might mean for navigational instruments. While it is recognized that the district shows attractive characteristics, the degree to which these inconsistencies straightforwardly correspond with vanishings stays a subject of continuous logical request. The connection between attractive irregularities and the revealed compass breakdowns requires a nuanced assessment that thinks about both normal varieties and innovative variables.

Navigational difficulties structure a basic part of the logical examination of the Bermuda Triangle. Pilots and sailors have announced cases of compass glitches, whimsical instrument readings, and bewilderment. The combination of navigational troubles across various methods of transportation brings up issues about the more extensive ramifications for sea and avionics wellbeing.

The logical focal point dives into the specialized parts of navigational instruments, trying to observe whether the detailed peculiarities are novel to the Bermuda Triangle or on the other hand assuming they line up with more extensive difficulties looked in different districts. By disconnecting the particular navigational difficulties inside the Bermuda Triangle, specialists expect to give a more clear comprehension of the dangers related with crossing this region.

In looking at the logical parts of the Bermuda Triangle, it is urgent to address the common hypotheses and legends that have encircled the area. Extraterrestrial association, time travels, and submerged urban communities are among the speculative thoughts that have saturated mainstream society. The logical focal point, in any case, stresses the significance of observational proof and testable speculations. While these speculations might catch the creative mind, they come up short on groundwork of logical request and stay in the domain of fiction until validated by substantial proof.

The transaction among science and culture adds an interesting layer to the examination. Logical clarifications frequently coincide with social accounts that add to the Bermuda Triangle's persona. Fables, legends, and accounts of apparition delivers and reviled waters have been gone down through ages, molding impression of the area. The logical focal point recognizes the social aspect, perceiving that the human experience is entwined with both objective perceptions and abstract understandings. Overcoming any barrier between logical examination and social comprehension is fundamental for an all encompassing investigation of the Bermuda Triangle.

Headways in innovation have fundamentally affected the logical investigation of the Bermuda Triangle. Satellite symbolism, remote detecting innovations, and high level sonar frameworks offer new devices for checking the locale's elements. Satellites give constant information on weather conditions, ocean surface temperatures, and sea flows, empowering researchers to follow and dissect conditions inside the Bermuda Triangle. High level sonar frameworks work with submerged investigation, possibly revealing destruction or land includes that have evaded revelation previously. The marriage of innovation and logical request opens roads for a more nuanced and information driven comprehension of the district.

As the logical focal point keeps on zeroing in on the Bermuda Triangle, interdisciplinary cooperation becomes central. Oceanographers, meteorologists, geophysicists, and navigational specialists should work couple to disentangle the intricacies of the district. Incorporating discoveries from different fields of study adds to a thorough comprehension that goes past disengaged clarifications. The Bermuda Triangle, with its diverse difficulties, requests a methodology that rises above disciplinary limits and embraces the intrinsic intricacy of the regular world.

All in all, the logical focal point applied to the Bermuda Triangle attempts to demystify the conundrum through thorough request and proof based examination. Oceanography, meteorology, geophysics, and navigational sciences meet to give an extensive comprehension of the difficulties looked inside the locale. While the secrets of the Bermuda Triangle keep on enthralling the human creative mind, the logical focal point offers a pathway to isolate reality from fiction, giving bits of knowledge that add to a nuanced and informed talk on this persevering through puzzler.

The Logical Focal point Proceeded: A More profound Jump into Bermuda Triangle Conundrum

As the logical focal point examines the secrets of the Bermuda Triangle, it is critical to dig into the particular episodes that have added to the district's notorious standing. While established researchers stays committed to disentangling the puzzler, it is fundamental to inspect probably the most outstanding vanishings inside the Bermuda Triangle, utilizing a basic and proof based approach.

One of the notorious cases that has energized the Bermuda Triangle mythos is the vanishing of Flight 19 in December 1945. A group of five U.S. Naval force planes drove by Lieutenant Charles Taylor left on a normal preparation mission from the Maritime Air Station in Post Lauderdale, Florida. Reports demonstrate that the pilots experienced compass breakdowns, professed to be perplexed, and at last radioed that they couldn't decide their area. As fuel ran short, Flight 19 vanished suddenly.

The resulting search and salvage mission, known as Flight 19's "Lost Watch," experienced its own evaporating go about as a salvage plane likewise vanished suddenly. The logical investigation of this episode includes an assessment of the overarching weather patterns, navigational difficulties, and the exhibition of the airplane in question. While the vanishing stays unexplained, the logical focal point plans to observe whether regular variables or outside impacts assumed a part in the evaporating of Flight 19.

The Mary Celeste, albeit not straightforwardly inside the geological bounds of the Bermuda Triangle, is a phantom boat that adds an unpleasant aspect to the district's puzzler. Found loose in the Atlantic in 1872, the Mary Celeste was without its group, who appeared to have evaporated suddenly. The boat's freight, including significant liquor, was immaculate, and there were no indications of battle or pain. While the Mary Celeste's vanishing originates before the advancement of the Bermuda Triangle legend, it imparts similitudes to the stories related with the locale. The logical focal point inspects verifiable weather conditions, sea conditions, and the vessel's development to grasp the conditions that prompted the group's baffling vanishing.

The USS Cyclops, an epic U.S. Naval force freight transport, remains as quite possibly of the main maritime vanishing inside the Bermuda Triangle. In 1918, during The Second Great War, the USS Cyclops disappeared without a follow while on the way from Brazil to Baltimore. The boat, conveying a heap of manganese metal and more than 300 group individuals, never arrived at its objective. In spite of broad pursuit endeavors, no destruction or garbage was at any point found. The vanishing of the USS Cyclops stays one of the best oceanic secrets of the twentieth 100 years. Logical examination concerning this occurrence includes an investigation of the boat's primary uprightness, freight, and winning atmospheric conditions. The objective is to decide if normal variables or human-related issues added to the vanishing.

The Black magic, an extravagance yacht that evaporated in 1967, acquainted a cutting edge section with the Bermuda Triangle's list of vanishings. The yacht set out from Miami on a twilight night for a short voyage and bafflingly vanished in spite of being just a mile seaward and furnished with the most recent navigational innovation. The absence of misery signals, good atmospheric conditions, and the vicinity to the coast bewildered specialists. The logical focal point examines this episode through the crystal of mechanical headways and navigational hardware, expecting to comprehend whether the vanishing of the Black magic difficulties the supposition that advanced vessels are resistant to the secrets of the Bermuda Triangle.

The Bay Stream, a strong sea momentum moving through the Bermuda Triangle, has been embroiled in different vanishings. Its quick and tempestuous nature could add to the fast vanishing of destruction, making it trying for search and salvage groups to find trash. Also, the Bay Stream's impact on atmospheric conditions might prompt unexpected and savage tempests that could overpower vessels and airplane. The logical focal point surveys the job of the Bay Stream in unambiguous vanishings, breaking down the transaction between maritime elements and the detailed difficulties looked by sailors and pilots.

In dissecting the Bermuda Triangle through the logical focal point, it is significant to recognize the continuous discussions encompassing the different speculations endeavoring to make sense of the locale's secrets. Attractive oddities, submerged geology, and navigational difficulties are perceived highlights, however their immediate relationship with vanishings stays theoretical. The Bay Stream's part in vanishings adds a layer of intricacy, entwining maritime elements with stories of evaporated ships and planes. Hypotheses including extraterrestrial powers, time travels, and submerged urban areas need experimental proof and logical help.

Doubters contend that numerous occurrences inside the Bermuda Triangle can be credited to normal peculiarities, human mistake, or navigational difficulties, and that the area's standing is swelled by specific announcing and sentimentality. Defenders of paranormal clarifications, then again, fight that the sheer volume of unexplained vanishings inside the locale recommends the presence of remarkable and potentially powerful powers.

The logical focal point looks to explore through these differentiating viewpoints, depending on exact proof, thorough investigation, and the standards of logical request to recognize the variables adding to the Bermuda Triangle's secrets.

As innovative headways keep on molding logical investigation, devices like satellite symbolism, high level sonar frameworks, and further developed navigational instruments offer additional opportunities for examining the examples and shared characteristics related with missing boats and airplane. Remote detecting innovations take into consideration the deliberate observing of the locale's maritime and environmental circumstances, giving ongoing information that can add to a more nuanced examination of the Bermuda Triangle's elements. High level sonar frameworks empower specialists to dig into the profundities of the sea, possibly uncovering destruction or proof that has escaped revelation before. The coordination of innovation into logical request addresses a promising outskirts for acquiring further experiences into the secrets of the Bermuda Triangle.

4.1 Introduction to scientific theories explaining phenomena.

Prologue to Logical Speculations Making sense of Peculiarities: Unwinding the Texture of the Normal World

The logical strategy, with its establishment in exact perception, methodical trial and error, and proof based thinking, has been mankind's most powerful apparatus for grasping the multifaceted functions of the regular world. The quest for logical information has prompted the plan of various speculations that look to make sense of assorted peculiarities going from the minuscule cooperations at the quantum level to the amazing sizes of cosmology. This investigation into the domain of logical speculations is an excursion that divulges the magnificence and intricacy of the universe while giving a guide to understanding the basic standards overseeing our world.

At the core of logical request is the undertaking to comprehend the major powers and rules that administer the actual universe. From Newton's laws of movement to Einstein's hypothesis of relativity, logical speculations act as systems that sort out and make sense of noticed peculiarities. They are not changeless creeds but rather developing designs, dependent upon refinement and variation as new proof arises and innovation propels. The force of logical hypotheses lies in their capacity to anticipate, depict, and eventually upgrade our understanding of the regular world.

One of the foundation speculations in present day material science is quantum mechanics, a domain that dives into the way of behaving of particles at the littlest scales. Formed in the mid twentieth 100 years, quantum mechanics upset how we might interpret matter and energy. It presented ideas like wave-molecule duality, where particles like electrons show both molecule and wave-like attributes. Quantum entrapment, another exceptional perspective, depicts particles that become interwoven no matter what the distance between them.

The hypothesis' probabilistic nature challenges traditional thoughts of determinism, offering a probabilistic structure for foreseeing the results of molecule communications. As quantum mechanics proceeds to amaze and baffle, it highlights the requirement for new standards in figuring out the tiny texture of the real world.

In the domain of cosmology, the Theory of the universe's origin remains as the predominant clarification for the beginning and development of the universe. Proposed in the mid twentieth hundred years, the hypothesis sets that the universe started as a very hot and thick state around 13.8 quite a while back and has been extending from that point forward. The observational proof supporting the Theory of prehistoric cosmic detonation, including the grandiose microwave foundation radiation and the overflow of light components, has hardened its status as the main clarification for the universe's starting points. In any case, secrets continue, for example, the idea of dim matter and dim energy, which comprise most of the universe's mass-energy content. These puzzles feature the powerful idea of logical speculations, provoking continuous examinations to refine and grow how we might interpret grandiose peculiarities.

In science, the hypothesis of development by regular choice, proposed by Charles Darwin, remains as a stupendous clarification for the variety of life on The planet. Developmental hypothesis sets that species change over the long haul through the systems of normal choice, hereditary float, and transformation. The fossil record, relative life structures, and atomic science give undeniable proof supporting the interconnectedness of every living organic entity and their common developmental family. While the fundamental precepts of transformative hypothesis are broadly acknowledged, continuous exploration keeps on refining the subtleties and investigate extra factors adding to the intricacy of the developmental cycle.

Drawing nearer to Earth, the hypothesis of plate tectonics explains the unique cycles forming the planet's surface. Created during the twentieth hundred years, this hypothesis places that the World's lithosphere is partitioned into structural plates that float on the semi-liquid asthenosphere underneath them. The development and communications of these plates bring about peculiarities like tremors, volcanic action, and the arrangement of mountain ranges. The hypothesis of plate tectonics makes sense of geographical elements as well as gives experiences into the World's set of experiences, including the gathering and separation of mainlands more than great many years.

Environment science depends on the crucial standards of thermodynamics and liquid elements to clarify the perplexing connections administering Earth's environment framework. The nursery impact, a peculiarity made sense of by the ingestion and re-outflow of infrared radiation by ozone harming substances, shapes the reason for grasping the World's temperature guideline.

Logical models based upon these standards permit analysts to recreate and anticipate environment designs, evaluate the effects of human exercises on the environment, and form methodologies for moderating environmental change. The interdisciplinary idea of environment science features the interconnectedness of different logical disciplines in tending to complex certifiable difficulties.

Hereditary hypothesis, established in the standards of atomic science and heredity, has gone through groundbreaking headways in ongoing many years. The revelation of the design of DNA by James Watson and Francis Kink established the groundwork for understanding the hereditary code that oversees the legacy of attributes. The planning of the human genome, finished at the beginning of the 21st hundred years, opened extraordinary bits of knowledge into the complexities of human hereditary qualities. Hereditary hypotheses not just clear up the transmission of attributes from one age for the following yet additionally structure the reason for leap forwards in clinical examination, customized medication, and the expected control of hereditary material.

The Standard Model of molecule material science epitomizes our ongoing comprehension of rudimentary particles and their cooperations. Created all through the twentieth 100 years, this hypothesis characterizes particles like quarks, leptons, and bosons, giving an extensive system to grasping the subatomic world. The new revelation of the Higgs boson at the Huge Hadron Collider denoted a critical approval of the Standard Model. Nonetheless, the model isn't without its holes, leaving space for investigation into peculiarities like dull matter and the unification of essential powers. As physicists push the limits of information, they wrestle with questions that might require the advancement or development of existing hypotheses.

The logical strategy's iterative nature cultivates a constant course of speculation, trial and error, and refinement. Speculations act as temporary clarifications that endure investigation until new proof or bits of knowledge brief updates. The course of falsifiability, a foundation of logical request, expects that hypotheses be testable and dependent upon potential dismissal in light of exact proof. This self-remedying component recognizes science from creed, guaranteeing that how we might interpret the normal world develops pair with our ability for perception and investigation.

While logical speculations offer powerful systems for making sense of noticed peculiarities, they are not insusceptible to outlook changes. Thomas Kuhn's idea of logical unrests highlights that changes in central seeing frequently go with huge leap forwards. The Copernican unrest, which dislodged the Earth from the focal point of the universe, and the change from traditional to quantum mechanics are instances of such groundbreaking movements. Logical hypotheses, strong as they might be, exist inside a unique scene that energizes constant addressing and investigation.

Lately, the mission for a bound together hypothesis of everything has powered hypothetical material science. Researchers seek to join the unique domains of quantum mechanics and general relativity under a solitary, exquisite structure. String hypothesis, a hypothetical system setting that essential particles are minuscule, vibrating strings, addresses one road of investigation. While the mission for a brought together hypothesis stays continuous, the difficulties and intricacies of combining quantum mechanics and relativity feature the boondocks of logical request.

The transaction among perception and hypothesis in science represents the corresponding connection among understanding and clarification. As new observational devices, innovative headways, and interdisciplinary methodologies grow the skylines of logical investigation, hypotheses advance to oblige and make sense of arising peculiarities. The logical undertaking is certainly not a static pursuit yet a dynamic and cooperative cycle that rises above individual speculations, adding to a consistently developing embroidery of human information.

Taking everything into account, the prologue to logical speculations making sense of peculiarities mirrors the steady quest for understanding that characterizes the logical endeavor. From the tiny universe of quantum mechanics to the vast sizes of cosmology, logical speculations give systems to appreciating the normal world. These hypotheses, based on the mainstays of exact perception, trial and error, and falsifiability, epitomize the human ability to unwind the intricacies of the real world. As we leave on an excursion through the mind boggling scenes of logical speculations, we embrace the soul of request that impels mankind toward more profound bits of knowledge and a more significant comprehension of the universe.

4.2 Discussing natural explanations, magnetic anomalies, and geological features.

Talking about Regular Clarifications, Attractive Peculiarities, and Land Highlights: Disentangling the Puzzle of the Bermuda Triangle

The Bermuda Triangle, a district enveloping focuses in Miami, Bermuda, and Puerto Rico, has long enthralled the public creative mind because of its relationship with strange vanishings of boats and airplane. While fantastical hypotheses including extraterrestrial powers and heavenly peculiarities have penetrated mainstream society, a logical assessment underscores regular clarifications established in oceanography, geophysics, and meteorology. Among the different elements adding to the persona of the Bermuda Triangle, attractive peculiarities and geographical highlights arise as central marks of examination, revealing insight into the mind boggling interaction of normal powers inside this confounding span.

Oceanography, the investigation of the physical and natural properties of the sea, gives a fundamental comprehension of the unique powers at play inside the Bermuda Triangle. The district is navigated by the Inlet Stream, a strong sea momentum that streams from the Bay of Mexico into the North Atlantic. This quick and violent current impacts the region's hydrodynamics, making conditions that can be trying for sea route. The combination of numerous flows in the Bermuda Triangle adds to the development of eccentric and possibly risky circumstances for ships, including the event of maverick waves.

The Bay Stream, while fundamental for managing worldwide environment designs, can present navigational difficulties because of its fast stream and variable nature. Sailors exploring through the Bermuda Triangle might areas of strength for experience, choppiness, and moving water temperatures, factors that can add to the troubles looked by vessels in the locale. The regular clarification lies in the oceanographic qualities innate to the Bermuda Triangle, underscoring the requirement for a complete comprehension of the locale's hydrodynamics to securely explore its waters.

Meteorology, the investigation of the environment and its peculiarities, acquaints one more aspect with the normal clarifications related with the Bermuda Triangle. Abrupt and brutal tempests, driven by the assembly of exchange winds and the impact of the Bay Stream, are common in the locale. These meteorological peculiarities can make testing conditions for both sea and aeronautics exercises. The quick changes in weather conditions, combined with the potential for the arrangement of waterspouts and other environmental aggravations, add to the dangers looked by vessels and airplane navigating the Bermuda Triangle.

The interconnected idea of oceanography and meteorology inside the Bermuda Triangle highlights the significance of thinking about the district's climatic circumstances in any examination of baffling vanishings. Storm floods, high breezes, and tempestuous oceans created by barometrical aggravations can present huge dangers to ships, possibly prompting mishaps or sinkings. Additionally, avionics exercises inside the Bermuda Triangle are vulnerable to unexpected and serious weather conditions changes, affecting flight steadiness and security. The regular clarifications grounded in oceanography and meteorology feature the requirement for an all encompassing methodology that thinks about the exchange of climatic and maritime elements inside this novel topographical region.

Geophysics, the investigation of the World's actual properties and cycles, adds to the investigation of regular clarifications for peculiarities inside the Bermuda Triangle. Attractive inconsistencies, an irrefutable element of the locale, have been proposed as a component impacting navigational instruments and adding to the secretive vanishings. The World's attractive field shows anomalies inside the Bermuda Triangle, prompting varieties in compass readings.

Attractive irregularities result from vacillations in the World's attractive field, which can influence navigational instruments depending on attractive direction. Compass needles might act whimsically, pointing in eccentric headings or displaying peculiar vacillations. The effect of attractive inconsistencies on navigational instruments is a substantial and deductively recorded peculiarity, giving a characteristic clarification to revealed compass breakdowns inside the Bermuda Triangle.

While attractive oddities add to navigational difficulties, the immediate connection between's these irregularities and vanishings stays a subject of progressing logical request. The intricacy lies in knowing whether the noticed attractive varieties are causative elements or coincidental to the vanishings. Moreover, headways in navigational innovation have diminished the dependence on attractive instruments, moderating the possible effect of attractive oddities on present day vessels and airplane. The job of attractive peculiarities inside the Bermuda Triangle requires a nuanced assessment that thinks about both verifiable and innovative elements.

Land highlights inside the Bermuda Triangle, including submerged geology and remote ocean channels, add a layer of intricacy to the regular clarifications related with the locale. The ocean bottom in this space shows critical varieties inside and out, with submerged highlights that might present difficulties to route. Unexpected changes in submerged geology, like the presence of submerged mountains or channels, could add to the troubles looked by sailors.

While the topographical elements inside the Bermuda Triangle are interesting, laying out an immediate connection between these highlights and vanishings requires cautious investigation. High level sonar frameworks and submerged planning advances offer chances to investigate the ocean bottom and distinguish possible perils. Understanding the land attributes of the locale is fundamental for making exact navigational diagrams and upgrading security measures for vessels exploring through the Bermuda Triangle.

The intermingling of oceanography, meteorology, and geophysics inside the Bermuda Triangle features the multi-layered nature of the area's difficulties. Normal clarifications established in these logical disciplines give a system to understanding the intricacies of the Bermuda Triangle's elements. It is pivotal to perceive that the regular powers at play, while impressive, are not vindictive; rather, they highlight the significance of educated route and the mix regarding logical information into sea and aeronautics rehearses.

As opposed to the sensationalized stories of extraterrestrial inclusion or paranormal exercises, the accentuation on normal clarifications lines up with the standards of logical request. By investigating the oceanographic, meteorological, and geophysical parts of the Bermuda Triangle, specialists look to demystify the locale and dissipate unwarranted legends. The logical methodology energizes a sober and confirm based comprehension of the difficulties presented by this extraordinary geological region.

As innovation keeps on progressing, giving new apparatuses to perception and examination, mainstream researchers is ready to develop how its might interpret the Bermuda Triangle. Satellite symbolism, high level sonar frameworks, and further developed navigational instruments offer exceptional chances to screen and concentrate on the district's elements continuously. Interdisciplinary cooperation, including specialists in oceanography, meteorology, geophysics, and navigational sciences, is fundamental for unwinding the complexities of the Bermuda Triangle's puzzler.

Investigating Normal Clarifications, Attractive Peculiarities, and Land Highlights: A More profound Plunge into the Bermuda Triangle Mystery

As we dive further into the investigation of regular clarifications, attractive oddities, and geographical highlights inside the Bermuda Triangle, it becomes basic to take apart these components in a more nuanced way, recognizing their intricacy and likely interconnections. The multi-layered nature of the Bermuda Triangle's secrets requests a complete comprehension that incorporates different logical disciplines, uncovering an embroidery of normal powers that shape the elements of this cryptic locale.

Oceanography, the investigation of the sea and its unpredictable properties, offers a fundamental focal point through which we can get a handle on the difficulties presented inside the Bermuda Triangle. The Bay Stream, a prevailing sea momentum coursing through this locale, assumes a significant part in forming its hydrodynamics. While the Inlet Stream is a crucial part of the World's environment guideline framework, its quick stream and fierce nature can make tricky circumstances for oceanic exercises. Ships exploring through the Bermuda Triangle might fight major areas of strength for with and flighty water disturbance, factors that can add to episodes and mishaps.

Besides, the combination of numerous flows inside the Bermuda Triangle adds an extra layer of intricacy. The multifaceted dance of these flows can lead to rebel waves, capricious floods of water that can represent a huge danger to vessels. These strong waves, frequently arriving at remarkable levels, are equipped for inverting even enormous boats, adding to the locale's standing for unexpected and unexplained vanishings.

Meteorology, the investigation of climatic peculiarities, intensifies the complexities of the Bermuda Triangle. The area is famous for its abrupt and fierce tempests, filled by the intermingling of exchange winds and impacted by the Bay Stream. These environmental unsettling influences can make testing conditions for both sea and aeronautics exercises. The quick changes in weather conditions, combined with the likely development of waterspouts — a climatic peculiarity similar to cyclones over water — present components of capriciousness and peril.

The association among oceanography and meteorology inside the Bermuda Triangle features the requirement for a coordinated methodology in understanding the difficulties looked by vessels and airplane. Storm floods, high breezes, and tempestuous oceans produced by climatic unsettling influences can all in all add to the locale's risky climate. By perceiving the collaboration between these regular powers, we gain a more significant appreciation for the perplexing elements that characterize the Bermuda Triangle.

Geophysics, a discipline investigating the World's actual properties, assumes a pivotal part in unwinding the secrets of the Bermuda Triangle, especially from the perspective of attractive oddities. The World's attractive field displays abnormalities inside this district, prompting varieties in compass readings. Compass breakdowns revealed by sailors and pilots exploring through the Bermuda Triangle have been credited to these attractive abnormalities.

While the relationship between's attractive inconsistencies and navigational difficulties is recognized, the immediate connection between these oddities and vanishings stays a subject of progressing banter. The intricacies emerge from knowing whether these irregularities are causative elements or accidental to the vanishings. Mechanical progressions have diminished the dependence on attractive instruments in present day vessels and airplane, obscuring the once-clear association between attractive abnormalities and navigational challenges. By the by, the tenacious idea of detailed compass glitches highlights the requirement for proceeded with examination concerning the job of attractive inconsistencies inside the Bermuda Triangle.

Land highlights, including submerged geography and remote ocean channels, add one more layer to the normal clarifications related with the Bermuda Triangle. The ocean bottom in this area shows huge varieties top to bottom, with submerged highlights that might present difficulties to route. Unexpected changes in submerged geography, like the presence of submerged mountains or channels, could add to the troubles looked by sailors.

The geographical viewpoints inside the Bermuda Triangle bring up charming issues about the job of submerged highlights in oceanic occurrences. Might vessels at some point experience surprising snags underneath the surface, prompting mishaps and vanishings? High level sonar frameworks and submerged planning advances offer promising roads for investigating the ocean bottom, revealing insight into potential perils that might have escaped recognition before. By understanding the land attributes of the area, analysts mean to improve navigational wellbeing and moderate the dangers related with submerged highlights.

Interdisciplinary cooperation is fundamental in exhaustively tending to the secrets of the Bermuda Triangle. Oceanographers, meteorologists, geophysicists, and navigational specialists should team up to wind around together the different strings of regular powers at play inside this extraordinary geological region. The intricacies of the Bermuda Triangle request a comprehensive methodology that rises above disciplinary limits, recognizing the interconnectedness of maritime, climatic, and land elements.

As innovation keeps on progressing, giving new devices to perception and investigation, established researchers is ready to develop how its might interpret the Bermuda Triangle. Satellite symbolism, high level sonar frameworks, and further developed navigational instruments offer exceptional chances to screen and concentrate on the area's elements progressively. These innovative progressions enable scientists to accumulate information that can add to a more nuanced examination of the Bermuda Triangle's intricacies.

All in all, the investigation of normal clarifications, attractive peculiarities, and land highlights inside the Bermuda Triangle is a continuous excursion that requires fastidious assessment and interdisciplinary coordinated effort. By diving into the complexities of oceanography, meteorology, and geophysics, we gain significant experiences into the regular powers forming this cryptic area.

Perceiving the interconnected idea of these disciplines gives an establishment to demystifying the Bermuda Triangle and scattering unwarranted legends. As we explore the flows of request and examination, the regular clarifications arise as a convincing story grounded in logical comprehension, welcoming us to disentangle reality behind the cloak of hypothesis and legend that has covered this secretive span for quite a long time.

Chapter 5

Secrets of the Deep

Insider facts of the Profound: Uncovering the Secrets of the Sea's Pit

The profound sea, a domain covered in unending obscurity and secret, disguises mysteries that have enthralled human creative mind for quite a long time. As we set out on an excursion to investigate the insider facts of the profound, we are constrained to dig into the deep profundities, where daylight scarcely infiltrates, and pressure arrives at stunning levels. This strange world, generally unfamiliar and neglected, holds the way to grasping Earth's set of experiences, biodiversity, and the principal powers molding our planet.

At the core of the mysteries of the profound untruths the deep plain, an immense and level scope that covers a large part of the sea depths. This apparently ruined scene is home to a variety of particular and mysterious animals adjusted to endure outrageous circumstances. Life in the deep plain has developed to flourish in close frosty temperatures, complete haziness, and tensions that can surpass multiple times that at the surface. The variation of creatures to these cruel circumstances challenges our assumptions about the restrictions of life and features the versatility of nature even with misfortune.

One of the most charming occupants of the deep plain is the anglerfish, an animal that has become inseparable from the secrets of the profound. With its bioluminescent bait hanging before its mouth like a living casting pole, the anglerfish draws in prey in the murkiness. The interesting cooperative connection among male and female anglerfish, where the a lot more modest male wires with the female's body to turn into an extremely durable parasite, adds a layer of intricacy to the generally puzzling universe of the chasm.

The deep plain isn't absent any trace of land action. Submarine volcanoes, aqueous vents, and seamounts intersperse the sea floor, adding to the unique idea of the remote ocean climate. Aqueous vents, specifically, are desert springs of life in the pit, supporting environments energized by chemosynthesis as opposed to daylight.

These outrageous conditions, plentiful in minerals and overflowing with life, offer a brief look into the potential for extraterrestrial life in correspondingly brutal circumstances.

The investigation of the profound sea uncovers the mysteries of Earth's topographical cycles, including plate tectonics and the development of maritime outside layer. Subs and remotely worked vehicles (ROVs) outfitted with state of the art innovation empower researchers to investigate the remote ocean channels, where structural plates impact and dive into the World's mantle. The Mariana Channel, the most profound region of the planet seas, arrives at profundities of more than 36,000 feet (10,994 meters) and stays a point of convergence for logical investigation. Disentangling the secrets of the channels adds to how we might interpret Earth's land history and the powers that shape the planet's surface.

Past the deep plain and remote ocean channels, the secrets of the profound stretch out to the animals occupying the mesopelagic and bathypelagic zones, usually alluded to as the nightfall and 12 PM zones. These zones, portrayed by lessening daylight and expanding pressure, have a different exhibit of living things, a large number of which stay unseen or inadequately comprehended. The goliath squid, an unbelievable and tricky occupant of the profound, typifies the difficulties of concentrating on life forms right at home. Ongoing progressions in innovation, for example, remote ocean submarines outfitted with top quality cameras and bioluminescence-delicate apparatuses, offer phenomenal chances to archive and concentrate on these tricky animals.

Bioluminescence, a peculiarity where residing creatures produce light, is a typical quality among remote ocean occupants. This regular light showcase fills different needs, including correspondence, predation, and disguise. The complex examples and shades of bioluminescent living beings make a hypnotizing display in the inky obscurity of the profound sea. Concentrating on bioluminescence not just improves how we might interpret remote ocean nature yet additionally rouses progressions in bioimaging innovation and clinical exploration.

The profound sea likewise assumes a urgent part in managing Earth's environment. Sea flows, driven by temperature and saltiness inclinations, course heat all over the planet, impacting weather conditions and environment frameworks. The retention of carbon dioxide by remote ocean waters, a cycle known as carbon sequestration, mitigates the effects of human-initiated environmental change. Understanding the multifaceted associations between the profound sea and the environment is fundamental for creating systems to address environment related difficulties.

Mechanical developments, like independent submerged vehicles (AUVs) and modern sonar planning frameworks, engage researchers to investigate the insider facts of the profound with remarkable accuracy. These apparatuses work with the making of nitty gritty guides, permitting scientists to study ocean bottom geology, recognize aqueous vent destinations, and find beforehand obscure elements. The utilization of acoustic innovation empowers researchers to direct studies of marine existence without upsetting their regular way of behaving, giving significant bits of knowledge into the biodiversity of the profound sea.

In spite of mechanical headways, the difficulties of investigating the profound sea continue. Tension, haziness, and outrageous temperatures require the advancement of particular gear fit for enduring these circumstances. The investigation of the deep profundities requests fastidious preparation, interdisciplinary joint effort, and a pledge to ecological stewardship. As we open the privileged insights of the profound, moral contemplations become central to guarantee that logical request doesn't incidentally hurt the very biological systems we try to comprehend.

The profound sea, frequently alluded to as Earth's last boondocks, keeps on being a wellspring of motivation and interest. The secrets it holds — whether as unseen species, geographical peculiarities, or biological cooperations — spellbind the minds of researchers, adventurers, and the overall population the same. The significance of rationing this delicate environment becomes clear as human exercises, for example, remote ocean mining and environmental change, present likely dangers to the fragile equilibrium of life in the pit.

Investigating the Chasm: Revealing Further Mysteries of the Profound Sea

The appeal of the profound sea rises above its actual aspects, reaching out into the domains of science, folklore, and human creative mind. As we leave on a complete investigation of the insider facts of the profound, we dive into less popular features, complexities, and the continuous logical undertakings that enlighten this baffling pit.

Biodiversity in the Remote ocean:

The surprising biodiversity of the remote ocean has turned into a point of convergence for logical request and protection endeavors. Past the famous animals that catch public interest, like the epic squid or the tricky gulper eel, lie a variety of less popular creatures with extraordinary variations.

Remote ocean corals, for example, structure multifaceted environments, giving living spaces to different marine species. These corals, frequently sluggish developing and delicate, face dangers from human exercises, including base fishing and environmental change. Saving these sensitive biological systems is fundamental for protecting the rich biodiversity of the profound.

The idea of "biogeographic territories" in the remote ocean adds a layer of intricacy to how we might interpret its variety. Unmistakable areas display novel collections of species affected by elements like profundity, temperature, and geography. Investigating these biogeographic regions upgrades our capacity to distinguish and safeguard areas of high biodiversity. Preservation techniques, including the foundation of marine safeguarded regions, mean to moderate the effect of anthropogenic exercises on remote ocean environments.

Transformations to Outrageous Conditions:

Life in the remote ocean is described by outrageous circumstances, including extraordinary strain, cold temperatures, and close complete dimness. The transformations displayed by remote ocean living beings to flourish in this antagonistic climate keep on captivating researchers. Numerous species have advanced specific highlights, like bioluminescence, to explore and convey in the haziness. The improvement of huge eyes in specific remote ocean animals upgrades their capacity to distinguish bioluminescent signals and explore through the faintly lit waters.

The strain in the remote ocean increments by roughly one environment for each ten meters of profundity. Life forms living at incredible profundities have developed to endure these huge tensions, with variations like adaptable skeletons, compressible bodies, and concentrated compounds. The investigation of extremophiles — creatures flourishing in outrageous circumstances — gives bits of knowledge into the restrictions of life on The planet and the potential for life in extraterrestrial conditions.

Remote ocean Organisms and Biogeochemical Cycles:

Organisms, the concealed engineers of life, assume a pivotal part in remote ocean environments and worldwide biogeochemical cycles. The disclosure of microbial life flourishing around aqueous vents tested past thoughts of the reliance of life on daylight. These extremophilic microorganisms use the synthetic energy from vent liquids, a cycle known as chemosynthesis, to support complex biological systems without daylight.

Organisms in the remote ocean add to the cycling of fundamental components, including carbon, nitrogen, and sulfur. Understanding these biogeochemical cycles is essential for disentangling the interconnectedness of Earth's different biological systems. Remote ocean organisms additionally hold guarantee for biotechnological applications, with catalysts and mixtures adjusted to outrageous circumstances offering expected benefits in medication, industry, and ecological remediation.

Mechanical Advances in Remote ocean Investigation:

The investigation of the profound sea has gone through an upset with the improvement of trend setting innovations. Remotely Worked Vehicles (ROVs), Independent Submerged Vehicles (AUVs), and monitored submarines outfitted with top quality cameras and testing apparatuses empower researchers to concentrate on the remote ocean climate with uncommon accuracy. These mechanical wonders have given looks into the mystery lives of remote ocean organic entities, uncovering ways of behaving, associations, and environments that were once distant.

One eminent progression is the utilization of DNA examination to recognize remote ocean species. Natural DNA (eDNA) permits researchers to distinguish hints of hereditary material shed by living beings into the encompassing water. This painless procedure has demonstrated important for concentrating on subtle and delicate species without direct perception. As innovation keeps on advancing, the opportunities for remote ocean investigation extend, opening new wildernesses for disclosure.

Remote ocean Mining and Preservation Difficulties:

The remote ocean has turned into a wilderness for modern double-dealing, with developing interest in remote ocean digging for important minerals, for example, polymetallic knobs, ocean bottom gigantic sulfides, and cobalt-rich hulls. Be that as it may, the possible natural effects of remote ocean mining raise worries among researchers and hippies. The actual unsettling influence of the ocean bottom, the arrival of dregs, and the expected disturbance of remote ocean environments present huge difficulties to reasonable asset extraction.

Adjusting the requirement for asset improvement with natural preservation requires cautious thought and global collaboration. The Global Seabed Authority (ISA), laid out under the Unified Countries Show on the Law of the Ocean, assumes a significant part in controlling remote ocean mining exercises. Finding some kind of harmony between monetary interests and the safeguarding of the remarkable biological systems of the profound sea stays a complicated and progressing challenge.

Environmental Change and the Profound Sea:

The profound sea assumes a pivotal part in environment guideline, filling in as a vault for

intensity and carbon dioxide. Environmental change, driven by human exercises, is adjusting the states of the remote ocean. Warming sea temperatures, changes in sea dissemination, and modifications in supplement circulation influence remote ocean environments. Understanding the repercussions of environmental change on the profound sea is fundamental for anticipating and alleviating its consequences for worldwide environment frameworks.

Sea fermentation, a result of expanded carbon dioxide ingestion via seawater, represents a danger to remote ocean organic entities with calcium carbonate shells, including specific corals and mollusks. Observing these progressions and carrying out procedures to address environment related difficulties are basic parts of worldwide protection endeavors.

Instructive Effort and Public Commitment:

The privileged insights of the profound sea are not bound to mainstream researchers; they have a place with mankind in general. Instructive effort and public commitment drives assume a significant part in cultivating mindfulness, appreciation, and preservation of the remote ocean. Joint efforts between researchers, teachers, and news sources add to dispersing information and motivating interest in the secrets of the profound.

Oceanographic foundations, galleries, and research associations frequently participate in outreach exercises, giving instructive assets, facilitating public talks, and making vivid displays. Narratives and well known science programs further add to public figuring out, bringing the marvels of the remote ocean into lounge rooms all over the planet. Developing a feeling of stewardship for the profound sea guarantees that people in the future perceive its worth and significance for the prosperity of the planet.

Moral Contemplations and Dependable Investigation:

As we open the insider facts of the profound, moral contemplations should direct our investigation and abuse of this puzzling domain. Mindful natural practices, adherence to preservation standards, and the minimization of human effect are principal. The fragile harmony between logical request and natural protection requires a promise to moral lead in remote ocean investigation.

Global joint effort is fundamental in laying out rules and guidelines that oversee remote ocean exercises. A proactive way to deal with ecological administration, informed by logical examination, guarantees that the privileged insights of the profound are uncovered without compromising the trustworthiness of its biological systems. Moral contemplations reach out past logical examination to include modern exercises, the travel industry, and asset extraction, requesting an all encompassing and supportable way to deal with our connections with the profound sea.

All in all, the mysteries of the profound address a continuous investigation into the obscure, where every revelation opens new roads of request and brings up new issues. The profound sea, with its deep fields, strange animals, and land ponders, welcomes us to disentangle its intricacies and value the interconnectedness of Earth's assorted environments. As innovation progresses and our comprehension develops, the insider facts of the profound stay a demonstration of the versatility of life and the persevering through charm of the neglected. The excursion into the void proceeds, powered by interest, mechanical development, and a significant appreciation for the miracles that anticipate revelation in the sea's profundities.

5.1 Delving into underwater mysteries and geological formations.

Digging into Submerged Secrets and Land Arrangements: Unwinding Earth's Underwater Privileged insights

The submerged domain, concealed underneath the outer layer of the World's seas and oceans, holds a bunch of secrets and topographical developments that have long charmed researchers and voyagers the same. As we leave on an excursion to dig into the profundities of these underwater mysteries, we reveal a world molded by structural powers, etched by submerged flows, and occupied by different biological systems. From the frightful magnificence of remote ocean channels to the entrancing complexities of submerged caves, our investigation uncovers the geographical ponders and lowered secrets that characterize Earth's lowered scenes.

Submarine Volcanoes and Seamounts:

Underneath the outer layer of the seas, a powerful universe of volcanic movement shapes the ocean bottom. Submarine volcanoes, stowed away from view, add to the production of new maritime hull and assume a fundamental part in Earth's geophysical cycles. These submerged volcanoes can be found along mid-sea edges, where structural plates separate, as well as in volcanic curves where plates unite.

Seamounts, transcending submerged mountains ascending from the ocean bottom, are a particular element of submarine scenes. These land developments, frequently wiped out volcanoes, intersperse the deep fields, making shelters for marine life. The perplexing environments encompassing seamounts flourish because of supplement rich upwelling flows, cultivating biodiversity and supporting different species. The investigation of these ocean bottom elements offers experiences into Earth's geographical history and the interconnectedness of marine biological systems.

Remote ocean Channels:

Among the most strange and remarkable geographical arrangements in the submerged world are remote ocean channels. These monster abysses, plunging large number of meters underneath ocean level, are frequently connected with subduction zones, where one structural plate slides underneath another. The Mariana Channel, the most profound known channel on The planet, arrives at profundities surpassing 36,000 feet (10,994 meters) in the Challenger Profound.

Remote ocean channels harbor special biological systems adjusted to outrageous circumstances, including extreme strain and freezing temperatures. The investigation of these channels discloses species uniquely adjusted to the deep climate, giving important experiences into the restrictions of life on our planet. Logical undertakings, furnished with subs and remotely worked vehicles (ROVs), have wandered into the profundities of channels to concentrate on the geographical cycles forming these cryptic highlights.

Submerged Caverns and Karst Arrangements:

Past the open territories of the sea floor, submerged caves and karst developments add a layer of intricacy to the underwater scene. These lowered caves, cut by the constant activity of water throughout topographical time, make unpredictable organizations underneath the ocean bottom. The Yucatan Landmass' lowered caverns, known as cenotes, offer a striking illustration of submerged karst developments.

Investigating submerged caves presents remarkable difficulties and awards for researchers and cavern jumpers. These secret domains frequently house delicate environments, including endemic species adjusted to the low-light circumstances. The investigation of submerged caves gives significant data about land processes, ocean level changes, and the associations among underground and marine conditions. Moreover, the conservation of these fragile biological systems becomes fundamental to keep up with biodiversity and logical respectability.

Mid-Sea Edges and Aqueous Vents:

Mid-sea edges, extending across the sea floor, address zones where structural plates are spreading separated. These far reaching submerged mountain ranges, portrayed by volcanic movement, assume a pivotal part in the formation of new maritime hull. The investigation of mid-sea edges divulges the unique cycles molding the ocean bottom and offers bits of knowledge into the World's inner design.

Aqueous vents, related with mid-sea edges, are focal points of substance and organic action. These vents discharge mineral-rich liquids into the sea, making desert gardens of life in the remote ocean. The environments encompassing aqueous vents depend on chemosynthesis, a cycle where microbes convert synthetic compounds into energy, supporting different networks of life forms. The investigation of these outrageous conditions gives fundamental information about the flexibility of life in the most difficult circumstances on The planet.

Sedimentary Bowls and Mainland Racks:

While the vast sea frequently becomes the dominant focal point in conversations of submerged scenes, the mainland racks and sedimentary bowls along shorelines harbor their own land secrets. Sedimentary bowls aggregate layers of dregs throughout land time, safeguarding records of past ecological circumstances and the development of life. These bowls assume a vital part in understanding Earth's set of experiences and the powers that have formed its surface.

Mainland racks, shallow submerged expansions of landmasses, are key regions for marine biodiversity and financial exercises. These districts, where daylight infiltrates the water section, support dynamic environments and are home to urgent fisheries. Understanding the topographical cycles impacting mainland racks is fundamental for overseeing marine assets and tending to natural changes.

Corals and Submerged Designs:

Past geographical developments etched by structural powers, the sea floor is enhanced with many-sided coral reefs and submerged structures. Coral reefs, frequently alluded to as the rainforests of the ocean, are perplexing environments worked by the calcium carbonate skeletons of coral polyps. These lively and different biological systems give territory to incalculable marine species and add to the general wellbeing of the seas.

The investigation of submerged structures, like geographical arrangements and counterfeit reefs, uncovers the powerful connections among topography and sea life science. Fake reefs, made deliberately or incidentally through the sending of lowered structures like wrecks, become centers for marine life. Understanding the environmental effect of these submerged designs illuminates protection endeavors and marine asset the executives.

Topographical Powers and Maritime Flows:

Topographical powers and maritime flows are personally associated, forming the submerged scene and affecting the dispersion of marine life. Structural plate developments, driven by Earth's inward intensity, add to the arrangement of ocean bottom elements and the formation of sea bowls. The development of water masses, driven by temperature and saltiness slopes, impacts the dispersal of supplements and the relocation examples of marine species.

Submarine gulches, cut by submerged flows, address captivating land includes that slice through mainland retires and inclines. These gullies give conductors to supplement rich waters to arrive at the remote ocean, supporting different biological systems. The connections between geographical powers and maritime flows establish a dynamic and interconnected climate that shapes the submerged world.

Anthropogenic Effect on Submerged Topography:

Human exercises, going from asset extraction to contamination, apply a significant effect on submerged geography and environments. Remote ocean mining, an arising industry driven by the interest for uncommon minerals, raises worries about the natural results of upsetting the ocean bottom. The statement of plastic waste, oil slicks, and compound poisons further add to the corruption of submerged conditions.

Understanding the anthropogenic effect on submerged geography requires an exhaustive evaluation of the drawn out results of human exercises. Preservation measures, supportable asset the executives, and global joint effort are fundamental to moderate the unfriendly impacts of modern and business exercises in the seas.

Mechanical Headways in Submerged Investigation:

The investigation of submerged secrets and geographical developments has been extraordinarily improved by mechanical advancements. Submarines, ROVs, and AUVs furnished with cutting edge sensors and imaging frameworks empower researchers to study the ocean bottom with remarkable accuracy. High-goal sonar planning, 3D imaging, and natural DNA investigation add to how we might interpret submerged scenes and biological systems.

Satellite innovation likewise assumes a significant part in checking and concentrating on submerged topographical highlights. Remote detecting permits researchers to notice huge scope maritime cycles, for example, the development of structural plates and changes in ocean surface temperatures. The joining of satellite information with in-situ perceptions upgrades our capacity to appreciate the complicated cooperations inside the submerged climate.

Instructive Effort and Public Commitment:

Sharing the disclosures and marvels of submerged topography with the more extensive public is a fundamental part of progressing logical information and encouraging ecological mindfulness. Instructive effort drives, narratives, and intelligent shows add to public comprehension and enthusiasm for the secrets underneath the waves. Joint efforts between researchers, instructors, and news sources intensify the effect of submerged investigation, moving interest and stewardship.

Instructive projects frequently center around the significance of marine protection, the interconnectedness of Earth's frameworks, and the requirement for mindful ecological practices. By connecting with general society in the investigation of submerged secrets, researchers and teachers develop a feeling of miracle and obligation regarding the seas, empowering people to become advocates for marine preservation.

Future Outskirts in Submerged Investigation:

As we dig further into the mysteries of the submerged world, new wildernesses in investigation call. The improvement of trend setting innovations, like multitude mechanical technology, computerized reasoning, and submerged living spaces, holds guarantee for extending how we might interpret submerged secrets. Independent investigation vehicles, fit for exploring testing landscapes and leading complex logical examinations, open roads for concentrating on remote and unavailable regions.

The coordination of interdisciplinary examination, uniting geologists, scientists, oceanographers, and designers, is fundamental for tending to the complex idea of submerged investigation. Worldwide joint efforts, informed by moral contemplations and a promise to supportability, will shape the fate of submerged examination and protection endeavors.

All in all, digging into submerged secrets and topographical arrangements is a continuous journey that improves how we might interpret Earth's dynamic and interconnected frameworks. From the secret profundities of remote ocean channels to the multifaceted designs of coral reefs, the submerged world unfurls as an embroidery of geographical miracles and natural wonders. As innovation progresses and logical information extends, the secrets underneath the waves keep on spellbinding our creative mind and rouse an aggregate liability to protect the excellence and respectability of Earth's lowered scenes.

5.2 Exploration of the ocean floor and its potential impact on ships and planes.

The sea floor, an immense and secretive scope covering over 70% of the World's surface, stays perhaps of the least-investigated outskirts. Late headways in marine innovation and submerged investigation have energized a flood in how we might interpret the mind boggling topography and biological systems concealed underneath the waves. As we leave on the investigation of the sea depths, disentangling its insider facts, we should likewise consider the potential effect these revelations might have on the security and route of boats and planes crossing the world's seas.

Planning the Pit:

The most important phase in the investigation of the sea depths includes planning its geology with extraordinary detail. High-goal sonar frameworks, bathymetric planning, and satellite innovation have altered our capacity to make precise and complete guides of the ocean bottom. These guides uncover the multifaceted highlights of submerged mountain ranges, remote ocean channels, and mid-sea edges, giving important bits of knowledge into the topographical cycles molding the sea depths.

Exact planning of the sea depths is critical for safe route and oceanic activities. Nautical graphs, got from definite bathymetric information, guide ships through delivery paths, keeping away from submerged risks and guaranteeing the security of sea traffic. As innovation propels, the ceaseless refreshing of nautical graphs becomes fundamental to reflect changes in the sea floor's geography and further develop route exactness.

Submerged Volcanoes and Seamounts:

The disclosure of submerged volcanoes and seamounts adds a layer of intricacy to how we might interpret the sea depths. These lowered volcanic highlights, frequently stowed away from view, can present dangers to route because of the potential for hazardous emissions or the presence of strange pinnacles. Checking and concentrating on these geographically dynamic regions become basic for sea security.

Seamounts, submerged mountains ascending from the ocean bottom, can impact sea flows and marine life. While they make rich biological systems because of supplement upwelling, seamounts may likewise introduce difficulties for route. Delivers ignoring seamounts need to consider varieties in water profundity and potential choppiness brought about by submerged geography.

Remote ocean Channels and Subduction Zones:

Remote ocean channels, the most profound focuses on the sea depths, are related with subduction zones where structural plates meet. The investigation of these channels, for example, the Mariana Channel, offers important experiences into the World's geophysical cycles. Notwithstanding, the outrageous profundities and tensions of channels present difficulties for investigation and bring up issues about the effect of subduction zones on oceanic exercises.

Subduction zones can produce strong seismic tremors and tidal waves, affecting the wellbeing of route in neighboring areas. Understanding the geographical qualities of subduction zones is fundamental for surveying the expected dangers and executing powerful early admonition frameworks to safeguard ships, seaside networks, and flying courses.

Submerged Geohazards:

Investigation of the sea floor has uncovered the presence of submerged geohazards that can affect the wellbeing of oceanic and avionics tasks. Submarine avalanches, submerged seismic tremors, and the arrival of methane hydrates are among the geographical peculiarities that can present dangers to boats and planes. Distinguishing and moderating these dangers require an extensive comprehension of the intricate cooperations between geographical cycles and the marine climate.

Submarine avalanches, set off by variables like residue shakiness or seismic action, can produce torrents with extensive outcomes. Checking weak locales and executing early admonition frameworks are fundamental parts of guaranteeing sea wellbeing in regions inclined to submarine avalanches.

Navigational Difficulties and Attractive Irregularities:

The investigation of the sea depths has revealed attractive irregularities that can influence navigational instruments on boats and planes. Varieties in the World's attractive field, frequently connected with land highlights, can prompt errors in compass readings. Understanding and planning these irregularities are significant for safe route, particularly in locales where attractive aggravations are predominant.

The Bermuda Triangle, a district famous for unexplained vanishings of boats and planes, has been related with attractive inconsistencies. While logical examinations recommend that normal clarifications, for example, methane hydrate ejections, may add to episodes around here, the view of attractive abnormalities perseveres in mainstream society. Explaining the logical comprehension of attractive abnormalities is fundamental for dispersing fantasies and guaranteeing exact navigational practices.

Influences on Submerged Foundation:

The investigation of the sea floor has extended past logical examination to incorporate submerged foundation advancement. Subsea links, pipelines, and establishments for oil and gas investigation are turning out to be progressively pervasive. Understanding the geographical qualities of the sea depths is fundamental for planning and keeping up with hearty submerged foundation that can endure the difficulties presented by the marine climate.

Subsea links, which structure the foundation of worldwide correspondence organizations, require exact intending to keep away from geographical perils and guarantee their flexibility. Furthermore, seaward boring tasks for oil and gas extraction request a careful comprehension of the ocean bottom geography to relieve chances related with submerged geohazards.

Biological Contemplations:

Investigation of the sea depths raises environmental contemplations connected with the possible effect on marine life and submerged biological systems. Aggravations brought about by submerged mining, penetrating, or foundation improvement can have extensive ramifications for biodiversity. Adjusting the advantages of investigation with the conservation of sensitive marine conditions is an essential part of capable submerged research.

The Worldwide Seabed Authority (ISA) assumes a key part in controlling exercises connected with seabed mining and guaranteeing that investigation is directed in a naturally reasonable way. Cooperative endeavors between mainstream researchers, policymakers, and industry partners are fundamental to lay out rules that safeguard marine biological systems while considering dependable investigation of the sea floor.

Arising Advances in Sea Investigation:

Progressions in submerged advanced mechanics, independent vehicles, and sensor advancements have changed the scene of sea investigation. Remotely Worked Vehicles (ROVs) and Independent Submerged Vehicles (AUVs) furnished with modern imaging frameworks empower researchers to direct nitty gritty overviews of the sea depths. These advancements improve our capacity to investigate out of reach regions and accumulate high-goal information for land and ecological examinations.

Automated submerged vehicles likewise assume a part in examining and keeping up with submerged foundation. Their capacity to work at incredible profundities, endure high tensions, and explore complex territories makes them significant apparatuses for the assessment and fix of subsea links, pipelines, and different establishments.

Global Coordinated effort and Administration:

The investigation of the sea floor requires worldwide cooperation and administration to address the difficulties and open doors that emerge. The Unified Countries Show on the Law of the Ocean (UNCLOS) gives a structure to the guideline of exercises in worldwide waters, including the investigation of the seabed. The ISA, laid out under UNCLOS, manages the guideline of seabed mining in regions past public locale.

Worldwide cooperation cultivates the sharing of logical information, information, and best works on, adding to a more thorough comprehension of the sea floor. As investigation exercises extend, successful administration components become progressively essential to guarantee the economical and dependable utilization of marine assets.

Instructive Effort and Public Mindfulness:

Connecting with general society in the investigation of the sea depths is critical for building mindfulness, encouraging appreciation, and tending to confusions. Instructive effort projects, narratives, and public mindfulness crusades assume an essential part in conveying the significance of sea investigation and its effect on different parts of human existence, including transportation and route.

By conveying the logical revelations, difficulties, and advantages of sea investigation, these drives add to a more educated and ecologically cognizant worldwide local area. Public help for dependable investigation rehearses and reasonable approaches is instrumental in molding the eventual fate of sea investigation and its effect on oceanic and flying exercises.

Offsetting Investigation with Preservation:

The double test of propelling sea investigation while guaranteeing the preservation of marine environments requires a fragile equilibrium. Mindful investigation rehearses, moral contemplations, and adherence to natural guidelines are fundamental parts of accomplishing this equilibrium. Logical examination ought to be led in manners that limit aggravations to marine life and natural surroundings, and the discoveries ought to be utilized to illuminate protection endeavors.

Preservation drives, like the foundation of marine safeguarded regions, add to the protection of basic living spaces and biodiversity. Finding some kind of harmony among investigation and protection includes the coordinated effort of researchers, policymakers, industry partners, and people in general to foster maintainable practices that shield the strength of the seas.

All in all, the investigation of the sea floor opens new boondocks of information, offering experiences into the World's topography, biological systems, and likely assets. In any case, this investigation additionally delivers difficulties connected with route security, biological effects, and the capable utilization of marine assets. As innovation proceeds to progress and global coordinated effort extends, an amicable way to deal with sea investigation — one that offsets logical revelation with natural stewardship — is fundamental for exploring the profundities of disclosure and guaranteeing a feasible future for the seas and the planet.

Chapter 6

Conspiracies Afloat

Connivances Above water: Exploring the Waters of Oceanic Secrets and Unexplained Peculiarities

The oceanic domain, with its immense regions and mysterious profundities, has for quite some time been a favorable place for stories of secret, interest, and unexplained peculiarities. "Connivances Above water" dives into the shadowy waters where reality and fiction interlace, investigating oceanic secrets that have spellbound the human creative mind and led to an embroidery of paranoid fears. From evaporated vessels to spooky spirits, this investigation explores the waters of oceanic riddles, unwinding the strings of hypothesis that wind through the stories of the great oceans.

The Bermuda Triangle: A Ceaseless Riddle:

No investigation of oceanic secrets is finished without diving into the scandalous Bermuda Triangle. This approximately characterized area in the western piece of the North Atlantic Sea has been the focal point of endless paranoid notions, ascribing the vanishings of boats and airplane to everything from extraterrestrial impedance to submerged oddities. While logical clarifications frequently highlight regular peculiarities and human mistake, the Bermuda Triangle's persona perseveres in mainstream society.

Paranoid fears encompassing the Bermuda Triangle frequently include accounts of evaporated vessels, puzzling navigational breakdowns, and electronic interruptions. The getting through charm of this oceanic puzzle has roused a heap of books, narratives, and speculative conversations, adding to its status as an image of the unexplained in the records of sea history.

The Mary Celeste: Phantom Boat or Nautical Puzzle?

The tale of the Mary Celeste stays perhaps of the most persevering through oceanic secret. Found unfastened in the Atlantic Sea in 1872, the boat was absent any and all its group, without any indications of battle or pain. Speculations encompassing the Mary Celeste range from robbery and revolt to the ocean beasts and extraterrestrial snatching. Notwithstanding exhaustive examinations, the destiny of the group remains covered in vulnerability.

Connivances above water in regards to the Mary Celeste frequently estimate about the thought processes behind the group's vanishing. A few hypotheses propose treachery or mystery plans, while others engage the chance of paranormal intercessions. The persevering through interest with the Mary Celeste epitomizes how oceanic secrets can rise above their verifiable setting, catching the aggregate creative mind for ages.

The Philadelphia Trial: A Maritime Odyssey Through Time:

The Philadelphia Trial, a supposed maritime investigation directed during The Second Great War, has turned into a foundation of sea paranoid ideas. As per the story, the USS Eldridge, a maritime destroyer escort, was said to have been delivered imperceptible and magically transported from Philadelphia to Norfolk, Virginia. Reports of team individuals encountering mental and actual peculiarities have filled hypotheses about clandestine government tests in the domain of quantum physical science and trend setting innovation.

Intrigues above water with respect to the Philadelphia Trial dive into secret government projects, time travel, and interdimensional irregularities. While the authority position excuses the Philadelphia Examination as a lie, the story perseveres as a demonstration of the charm of sea tricks that stretch the limits of traditional comprehension.

The Apparition Boat of Northumberland Waterway:

The story of the Phantom Boat of Northumberland Waterway adds a ghostly aspect to sea secrets. As indicated by legend, a spooky vessel, enlightened by a ghostly green light, torment the waters off Ruler Edward Island. Witnesses have revealed sightings of the ghost transport, crediting its appearance to powerful powers or the waiting spirits of an unfortunate oceanic episode.

Schemes above water concerning phantom ships frequently include sea misfortunes and lost spirits sentenced to explore the oceans forever. The Apparition Boat of Northumberland Waterway joins the positions of otherworldly stories that obscure the lines between oceanic legends and unexplained peculiarities, welcoming hypothesis about the extraordinary powers at play on the high oceans.

The Flying Dutchman: Oceanic Old stories Takes Off:

The legend of the Flying Dutchman addresses a centuries-old oceanic secret saturated with old stories. The ghastly boat, reviled to cruise the oceans forever, has turned into a persevering through image of sea strange notion. Hypotheses encompassing the Flying Dutchman frequently investigate subjects of heavenly discipline, destined journeys, and the results of opposing the normal request.

Intrigues above water in regards to the Flying Dutchman rise above the limits of the real world, diving into the domains of the powerful and the mystical. The spooky ghost of the reviled transport keeps on catching the human creative mind, moving stories, craftsmanships, and variations in different types of media.

The Lost City of Atlantis: Underneath the Floods of Hypothesis:

While not solely a sea secret, the lost city of Atlantis has for quite some time been related with baffling undersea domains. Depicted by the old Greek savant Plato, Atlantis is said to have been a strong and high level human progress that evaporated underneath the waves. Intrigues above water with respect to Atlantis range from theories about its genuine presence to hypotheses about its trend setting innovation and asserted associations with extraterrestrial creatures.

The appeal of Atlantis stretches out past verifiable interest, rousing incalculable speculations about its area, downfall, and possible effect on mankind's set of experiences. Oceanic paranoid ideas frequently interlace with the more extensive account of Atlantis, making an embroidery of speculative narrating that joins components of paleontology, folklore, and pseudoscience.

The USS Cyclops: Evaporated Suddenly:

The vanishing of the USS Cyclops during The Second Great War stays quite possibly of the most baffling oceanic secret in maritime history. The collier transport, with a group of more than 300, evaporated without a follow in the Bermuda Triangle in 1918. Intrigues above water with respect to the USS Cyclops incorporate speculations about foe assaults, secret activities, and otherworldly peculiarities.

The USS Cyclops has turned into an image of the vulnerabilities that cover oceanic vanishings. While true examinations highlight the chance of mechanical disappointment or unfavorable weather patterns, the absence of indisputable proof has energized hypotheses about additional evil powers at play.

Submerged Peculiarities and Unexplained Peculiarities:

Tricks above water in the sea domain stretch out past unambiguous occurrences to envelop a more extensive range of submerged irregularities and unexplained peculiarities. From supposed submerged UFO bases to puzzling sonar readings and strange remote ocean structures, the profundities of the seas have become ripe ground for hypothesis and paranoid fears.

Hypotheses in regards to submerged peculiarities frequently meet with more extensive stories of extraterrestrial appearances, government smoke screens, and the presence of antiquated developments underneath the waves. The endlessness and unavailability of the sea floor add to the steadiness of intrigues above water, as the profundities remain generally neglected, leaving space for creative understandings and speculative narrating.

Government Mysteries and Grouped Missions:

Tricks above water in the oceanic area every now and again include government mysteries and grouped missions. Theories about secretive maritime tasks, trial innovations, and secret plans add to an environment of doubt and interest. From supposed submerged research offices to surreptitious military activities, sea paranoid notions frequently bring out subjects of mystery and government smoke screens.

Hypotheses in regards to government contribution in sea secrets range from doubts about the concealment of data to charges of agreement with extraterrestrial substances. The smoke screen that frequently encompasses military and government exercises adrift gives prolific ground to the development of schemes above water, where the obscure turns into a favorable place for hypothesis.

Exploring Truth and Fiction: The Test of Sea Tricks:

Isolating truth from fiction in the domain of sea tricks represents an extraordinary test. The sea space, tremendous and generally unfamiliar, offers a material whereupon fantasies, legends, and speculative stories can flourish. While a few oceanic secrets have been exposed or made sense of through logical request, others endure as strange riddles that keep on motivating theory.

The charm of sea connivances lies in their capacity to take advantage of the base apprehension about the obscure, the endlessness of the seas, and the secrets concealed underneath the waves. Tricks above water act as wake up calls, wellsprings of diversion, and, on occasion, impressions of cultural tensions and vulnerabilities.

The Social Effect of Sea Connivances:

Past their singular stories, sea connivances have a significant social effect. They shape the manner in which social orders see the ocean, filling a feeling of marvel, dread, and interest. Whether through writing, film, or well known fables, oceanic tricks add to the development of stories that rise above the limits of the real world.

The persevering through prominence of oceanic tricks in mainstream society highlights their reverberation with human brain research and the immortal appeal of the unexplored world. As these stories keep on catching the creative mind, they become an indispensable piece of the social embroidered artwork, impacting how we see the tremendous and strange fields of the world's seas.

The Job of Distrust and Decisive Reasoning:

While sea connivances might add a component of energy and interest to how we might interpret the oceans, a solid portion of incredulity and decisive reasoning is fundamental. Thorough logical request, proof based examination, and the use of Occam's razor — favoring less difficult clarifications over tangled tricks — are significant for exploring the waters of sea secrets.

Distrust welcomes us to scrutinize the accounts encompassing oceanic tricks, assess the believability of sources, and look for logical clarifications grounded in exact proof. By cultivating a culture of decisive reasoning, we can recognize between certified secrets that merit investigation and unwarranted schemes that might sustain falsehood.

The Eventual fate of Sea Secrets:

As innovation progresses and our comprehension of the seas develops, the fate of oceanic secrets holds guarantee for proceeded with investigation and revelation. Logical undertakings, outfitted with cutting edge apparatuses and advances, will disclose the privileged insights of the ocean, demystifying a portion of the long-standing mysteries that have filled sea tricks.

The convergence of sea life science, innovation, and investigation will assume a urgent part in molding the stories encompassing sea secrets. As we explore the oceans representing things to come, the limits among reality and fiction in sea schemes will keep on advancing, mirroring our steadily growing information on the seas and the persevering through human interest with the secrets that lie underneath the surface.

All in all, "Schemes Above water" welcomes us to leave on an excursion through the sea secrets that have caught our aggregate creative mind. Whether established in verifiable occurrences, old stories, or the unfamiliar profundities of the seas, these connivances above water address the persevering through human craving to investigate, comprehend, and, on occasion, decorate the secrets that the ocean holds. As we explore the waters of sea conundrums, let us approach them with a feeling of interest, doubt, and an appreciation for the significant effect they have on our social stories and our relationship with the tremendous and strange seas that characterize our planet.

6.1 Unraveling popular conspiracy theories surrounding the Bermuda Triangle.

Unwinding Well known Paranoid fears Encompassing the Bermuda Triangle: Isolating Reality from Fiction

The Bermuda Triangle, an inexactly characterized district in the western piece of the North Atlantic Sea, has been a hotbed of hypothesis, interest, and secret for a really long time. The region, generally limited by focuses in Miami, Bermuda, and Puerto Rico, has acquired reputation because of a progression of episodes including the vanishing of boats and airplane. While a large number of these occurrences have been made sense of by normal peculiarities and human mistake, the Bermuda Triangle keeps on being a point of convergence for paranoid notions that reach from the conceivable to the fantastical. In this investigation, we disentangle probably the most famous paranoid notions encompassing the Bermuda Triangle, looking at their beginnings, validity, and the logical clarifications that balance the charm of the secretive.

Extraterrestrial Kidnapping and UFO Contribution:

One of the persevering through paranoid fears encompassing the Bermuda Triangle recommends extraterrestrial contribution in the vanishings of boats and airplane. Defenders of this hypothesis guarantee that unidentified flying articles (UFOs) are liable for the baffling vanishings, either through kidnapping or the utilization of cutting edge innovations. The possibility that outsiders are involving the Bermuda Triangle as a base for their tasks adds a layer of sci-fi to the secret.

While the idea of extraterrestrial inclusion catches the creative mind, logical clarifications highlight more everyday causes. Numerous episodes in the Bermuda

Triangle can be ascribed to navigational mistakes, abrupt tempests, or mechanical disappointments. The shortfall of substantial proof supporting the extraterrestrial hypothesis consigns it to the domain of hypothesis as opposed to a trustworthy clarification for the strange events.

Time Travels and Vortex Peculiarities:

Paranoid notions including time travels, wormholes, or vortex peculiarities suggest that the Bermuda Triangle is a door to different aspects or periods in time. As per this account, boats and airplane entering these puzzling gateways wind up shipped to substitute real factors or verifiable times, adding to their evident vanishings. This hypothesis mixes components of sci-fi with the unexplained idea of the Bermuda Triangle.

Logically, time travels or vortex peculiarities needs observational help. The laws of material science, as presently comprehended, don't give a premise to such peculiarities in the regular world. Besides, nitty gritty examinations concerning the occurrences in the Bermuda Triangle commonly uncover regular clarifications established in atmospheric conditions, human blunder, or specialized breakdowns.

Submerged Atlantis Innovation and Old Secrets:

Paranoid fears connecting the Bermuda Triangle to the lost city of Atlantis suggest that cutting-edge antiquated innovation lies concealed underneath the sea's surface. As per this account, remainders of Atlantean human advancement, including strong energy sources or innovation outside our ability to comprehend, cause disturbances in the locale, prompting the puzzling vanishings. This hypothesis benefits from the persevering through interest with the incredible Atlantis and its implied innovative ability.

While the narrative of Atlantis adds a charming verifiable aspect to the Bermuda Triangle secret, standard paleohistory and geography have not validated the presence of a high level old progress in the district. Logical examinations focus on proof based approaches, and the absence of observational help for submerged Atlantis innovation consigns this hypothesis to the domain of speculative fiction.

Methane Hydrate Ejections and Gas-Related Occurrences:

A more grounded, yet still speculative, hypothesis suggests that methane hydrate ejections from the sea depths add to the baffling events in the Bermuda Triangle. Methane hydrates are ice-like designs that trap methane gas underneath the seabed. As indicated by this hypothesis, unexpected arrivals of methane air pockets could diminish the lightness of boats, prompting their sinking, or cause touchy occasions that jeopardize airplane.

While methane hydrate ejections are known to happen in a few maritime locales, the absence of significant proof associating these occasions to Bermuda Triangle vanishings debilitates the believability of the hypothesis. Besides, numerous occurrences in the area have more conceivable clarifications, like human blunder, gear disappointment, or antagonistic weather patterns.

Electromagnetic Oddities and Compass Deviation:

Paranoid fears including electromagnetic peculiarities propose that uncommon attractive fields in the Bermuda Triangle make compasses glitch, prompting navigational confusion. This hypothesis frequently focuses to compass varieties and electronic breakdowns announced by pilots and mariners as proof of strange powers at play in the area.

Experimentally, the World's attractive field isn't static, and varieties in attractive power are regular events. The Bermuda Triangle is one of a few regions on Earth where the attractive field acts in an unexpected way, yet these varieties are legitimate and don't represent a danger to present day route frameworks. While compass deviation is a genuine peculiarity, crediting it exclusively to paranormal or puzzling causes distorts the perplexing collaborations between attractive fields and route hardware.

Government Trials and Military Inclusion:

Paranoid notions including government tests and military association place that undercover exercises in the Bermuda Triangle are answerable for the secretive vanishings. Hypotheses range from clear-cut advantages testing to the improvement of cutting edge innovations that accidentally influence boats and airplane working in the area. This account plays into more extensive doubts about government mystery and surreptitious activities.

While it is actually the case that tactical exercises have happened nearby the Bermuda Triangle, crediting all vanishings to clandestine government tests needs significant proof. By far most of episodes can be made sense of through ordinary means, and there is restricted observational help for the idea that tactical exercises are efficiently causing these occasions.

Navigational Blunders and Human Elements:

One of the more practical clarifications for episodes in the Bermuda Triangle focuses on navigational mistakes and human variables. Defenders of this hypothesis contend that the locale's remarkable geographic elements, joined with testing weather conditions, add to challenges in route. Human mistakes, like distortion of instruments, weariness, or absence of involvement, assume a critical part in oceanic and flight occurrences.

Experimentally, examinations concerning Bermuda Triangle episodes frequently uncover a mix of navigational mistakes, climate related difficulties, and human variables. Exact route in the district requires a sharp comprehension of nearby circumstances, and inability to represent these variables can prompt surprising and possibly perilous circumstances.

Normal Peculiarities and Maverick Waves:

Paranoid fears including regular peculiarities, for example, rebel waves, violent flows, and unexpected tempests, recognize the difficulties presented by the area's dynamic climate. As indicated by this account, strong regular powers can overpower boats and airplane, prompting their vanishing. This hypothesis lines up with logical clarifications that focus on the comprehension of the area's remarkable weather conditions and maritime circumstances.

Deductively, the Bermuda Triangle is inclined to unusual climate peculiarities, including abrupt and extreme tempests. Maverick waves, which can arrive at stunning levels, are archived events in the district. While these normal variables add to the difficulties of route, they don't need summoning paranormal or extraterrestrial clarifications to represent sea episodes.

Media Sentimentality and Tendency to look for predetermined feedback:

A more basic viewpoint on Bermuda Triangle paranoid notions underlines the job of media drama and tendency to look for predictable feedback in sustaining the secret. The contention here is that high-profile occurrences get lopsided consideration, adding to a slanted impression of the district's risk. Preference for non threatening information, where occurrences that fit the Bermuda Triangle story are stressed while those with traditional clarifications are ignored, further builds up the secret.

Logically, an extensive examination of episodes in the Bermuda Triangle requires thinking about every single accessible datum and perceiving that the locale isn't intrinsically more risky than other vigorously voyaged sea regions. Media sentimentality can contort public insight, and a reasonable assessment of the proof uncovers that numerous occurrences have normal and logically upheld clarifications.

Exploring the Waters of Doubt and Request:

In unwinding the well known paranoid ideas encompassing the Bermuda Triangle, it becomes obvious that the appeal of the secretive frequently eclipses the more commonplace, yet deductively grounded, clarifications for oceanic and flight episodes in the locale. While the Bermuda Triangle has caught the public's creative mind for a really long time, isolating truth from fiction requires a pledge to doubt, decisive reasoning, and a dependence on proof based request.

Logical examinations concerning individual occurrences have reliably uncovered customary clarifications established in navigational difficulties, climate peculiarities, and human variables. The total load of observational proof backings the end that the Bermuda Triangle, while one of a kind in its geographic and air qualities, is definitely not an otherworldly or paranormal risk zone.

As we explore the waters of distrust and request, it is fundamental to perceive the effect of media stories, tendency to look for predictable feedback, and the persevering through allure of secret in molding public discernment. The Bermuda Triangle fills in as a wake up call about the force of narrating, the charm of the obscure, and the requirement for logical thoroughness in grasping the intricacies of our reality.

Without substantial proof supporting extraterrestrial contribution, time travels, or old civic establishments underneath the waves, the Bermuda Triangle stays a demonstration of the getting through human interest with secret and the neglected corners of our planet. While paranoid notions might add a component of fervor to the account, the logical strategy stays the most solid compass for exploring the waters of the obscure and unwinding the secrets that enrapture our aggregate creative mind.

6.2 Analyzing the role of media and popular culture in shaping perceptions.

Dissecting the Job of Media and Mainstream society in Forming Discernments: Exploring the Impact of Symbolism and Stories

Media and mainstream society assume a significant part in forming discernments, impacting how people see their general surroundings and decipher complex issues. The interweaving of media and culture makes a strong power that molds cultural mentalities, convictions, and values. This investigation dives into the complex manners by which media and mainstream society shape discernments, inspecting the effect of symbolism, accounts, and narrating on the shared perspective.

The Force of Symbolism: Molding Visual Accounts:

Pictures hold an exceptional power in forming discernments, frequently talking stronger than words. Visual stories, passed on through photos, delineations, and recordings, significantly affect how people decipher data. News sources and mainstream society substances influence this power, decisively choosing and introducing symbolism to inspire explicit feelings, pass on messages, and impact general assessment.

For instance, news inclusion depends intensely on visuals to convey the instantaneousness and effect of occasions. A painstakingly picked photo can evoke compassion, flash shock, or casing a story in a specific light. Likewise, mainstream society, including films, TV programs, and commercials, utilizes visual narrating to make close to home associations with crowds and engraving specific pictures onto the aggregate mind.

The impact of symbolism stretches out past news and diversion to shape view of cultural standards, excellence principles, and social assumptions. Commercials, specifically, add to building beliefs of engaging quality, achievement, and satisfaction, affecting how people see themselves as well as other people. The omnipresence of visual substance in the advanced age enhances its effect, as pictures become necessary to the development of reality in the personalities of the crowd.

Accounts and Narrating: Creating Social Stories:

Accounts, passed on through narrating in different structures, are instrumental in molding discernments and developing social personalities. Whether through news reports, writing, movies, or web-based entertainment, accounts make structures through which people figure out the world. The choice of characters, plotlines, and subjects adds to the development of social stories that reflect and shape cultural qualities.

In the domain of information media, the outlining of stories impacts how occasions are seen. News sources come to publication conclusions about which parts of a story to feature, the language utilized, and the setting gave. These decisions add to the making of accounts that can impact popular assessment, political talk, and social perspectives. The peculiarity of "plan setting" features how media accounts can focus on specific issues, forming the public's impression of what is critical or newsworthy.

Mainstream society, including writing, movies, and TV, assumes an essential part in developing social stories that impact cultural standards and assumptions. The portrayal of assorted characters, connections, and encounters adds to the standardization of specific points of view while underestimating others. For instance, the depiction of orientation jobs, race, and character in famous media shapes cultural assumptions and impacts how people see themselves as well as other people.

Social Authority and Philosophical Impact:

Media and mainstream society can sustain social authority by supporting prevailing belief systems and power structures. Social authority, an idea presented by Italian scholar Antonio Gramsci, alludes to the strength of a specific social perspective that serves the interests of the decision class. With regards to media, this idea appears in the ways in which certain stories, values, and points of view are special over others, frequently lining up with winning cultural standards.

The support of social authority through media can add to the minimization of minority voices and viewpoints. Generalizations, figures of speech, and one-sided depictions in media can propagate prejudicial mentalities and support existing power uneven characters. Perceiving and testing these examples is fundamental for encouraging inclusivity, variety, and a more fair portrayal of various characters and encounters.

Philosophical impact is especially obvious in political talk, where news sources and mainstream society elements might line up with explicit political belief systems. This arrangement can add to the polarization of general assessment and the entrenchment of philosophical partitions. The outlining of policy driven issues, determination of sources, and article choices impact how crowds decipher and answer political stories.

Virtual Entertainment and the Democratization of Stories:

The ascent of virtual entertainment has changed the scene of story development and data spread. Virtual entertainment stages engage people to take part in molding stories, giving a stage to different voices and points of view. The democratization of narrating via online entertainment challenges conventional media guardians and permits minimized networks to enhance their stories.

Nonetheless, the decentralized idea of web-based entertainment likewise presents difficulties. The spread of deception, closed quarters, and the quick scattering of unconfirmed stories add to a mind boggling media scene. The viral idea of specific stories via virtual entertainment can shape discernments and impact general assessment, now and again autonomous of real exactness.

Furthermore, calculations utilized by web-based entertainment stages assume a huge part in molding the substance people experience. These calculations, intended to expand commitment, can add to the arrangement of channel bubbles, where clients are presented to data that lines up with their current convictions. This specific openness can support previous insights and limit openness to assorted viewpoints.

Media Education and Basic Utilization: Exploring the Data Scene:

The complicated exchange among media and mainstream society highlights the significance of media proficiency and basic utilization. Media proficiency includes the capacity to examine, assess, and fundamentally draw in with media content. In a time of data over-burden, creating media education abilities is vital for exploring the subtleties of accounts, perceiving predisposition, and knowing among solid and questionable sources.

Instructive drives pointed toward upgrading media education enable people to dismantle media messages, figure out the components of story development, and recognize possible wellsprings of predisposition. By encouraging decisive reasoning abilities, media proficiency prepares people to explore the data scene, question presumptions, and draw in with media content in an insightful way.

Advancing media education likewise includes empowering a consciousness of the moral contemplations associated with media creation. This incorporates a comprehension of the effect of melodrama, the potential for hurt through the spread of deception, and the obligation of media elements to maintain editorial respectability. Moral media rehearses add to an additional straightforward and responsible media environment.

The Effect on General Assessment and Social Change:

The molding of discernments through media and mainstream society has unmistakable ramifications for popular assessment and cultural perspectives. Media accounts can impact public opinion on issues like governmental issues, civil rights, and social standards. The depiction of specific gatherings or issues in media can add to the forming of public perspectives, influencing strategy choices and cultural talk.

The potential for media and mainstream society to drive social change is exemplified by developments that influence narrating to bring issues to light and assemble support. Crusades revolved around issues like social equality, ecological protection, and orientation correspondence use stories to create compassion, move activity, and challenge cultural standards. The force of narrating to bring out close to home reactions and cultivate associations is a main impetus behind the capacity of media and culture to catalyze change.

On the other hand, the propagation of hurtful generalizations or one-sided stories in media can block progress toward a more comprehensive and fair society. Media portrayals add to the development of normal practices, and when these portrayals build up unfair mentalities, they can obstruct endeavors to accomplish civil rights.

Globalization and Social Trade:

The interconnectedness of the advanced world, worked with by globalization, has prompted expanded social trade through media and mainstream society. The spread of movies, network shows, music, and computerized content rises above public boundaries, impacting discernments on a worldwide scale. This trade of social items adds to the development of a globalized mainstream society that shapes shared values and impacts social personalities.

Nonetheless, the course of globalization likewise brings up issues about social colonialism and the predominance of specific social accounts over others. The exportation of Western media and social items, specifically, thely affects nearby societies and the likely eradication of different voices. Exploring the elements of social trade requires a familiarity with power lopsided characteristics and a guarantee to advancing social variety and portrayal.

Exploring the Media and Culture Nexus:

In the unpredictable transaction among media and mainstream society, the molding of discernments arises as a dynamic and persuasive cycle. The force of symbolism, the development of accounts, and the democratization of narrating through web-based entertainment altogether add to the intricate woven artwork of impacts that form cultural perspectives.

Understanding the job of media and mainstream society in forming discernments requires a nuanced approach that thinks about the effect on different networks and personalities. From the depiction of minimized gatherings to the effect on political talk, media education arises as a critical device for exploring the intricacies of the data scene.

As people draw in with media and social substance, developing decisive reasoning abilities becomes fundamental. Perceiving the potential for predisposition, addressing presumptions, and looking for different points of view add to a more educated and knowing way to deal with media utilization. Furthermore, advancing moral media practices and supporting drives that intensify underrepresented voices add to an additional comprehensive and fair media environment.

All in all, the nexus of media and mainstream society is a strong power that both reflects and shapes cultural discernments. Exploring this unique scene requires a continuous obligation to media education, basic utilization, and an acknowledgment of the significant effect that stories and symbolism have on the shared mindset. As we draw in with media and culture, we assume a functioning part in forming the accounts that characterize our common perspective of the world.

Chapter 7

Navigating the Unknown

Exploring the Unexplored world: An Excursion into the Strange Domains of Investigation and Disclosure

The human soul has forever been attracted to the appeal of the obscure, coaxing us to investigate, find, and unwind the secrets that lie past the recognizable. "Exploring the Unexplored world" epitomizes the substance of this persistent mission for information and experience, as people and social orders leave on ventures into unknown domains — both physical and figurative. This investigation dives into the diverse elements of exploring the obscure, from the domains of science and geology to the neglected regions of the psyche and the secrets that enamor the human creative mind.

The Call of Investigation: Planning the Strange Regions:

From the earliest nautical undertakings to contemporary space investigation, the call of investigation has driven humankind to wander into the unexplored world. The unfamiliar domains of the Earth and past entice adventurers to outline new guides, find stowed away scenes, and grow the limits of human information.

The soul of investigation has taken us from the profundities of the sea to the levels of the universe, stretching the boundaries of what we can fathom and accomplish.

By and large, adventurers like Christopher Columbus, Ferdinand Magellan, and Lewis and Clark explored strange waters and planned new terrains, opening up the world to additional revelation. In the advanced period, space organizations, for example, NASA have pushed mankind into the universe, sending tests to far off planets and satellites to the edges of our planetary group. The desire to investigate, energized by interest and the longing for figuring out, stays a main impetus in the human experience.

Logical Request and the Outskirts of Information:

Logical request fills in as a strong vessel for exploring the obscure, unwinding the secrets of the normal world and pushing the limits of information. From the tiny domains of quantum physical science to the vast spans of astronomy, researchers leave on scholarly excursions into neglected regions. The logical strategy gives a precise way to deal with figuring out the obscure, with trial and error, perception, and examination filling in as navigational devices.

In fields like hereditary qualities, neuroscience, and natural science, specialists explore strange domains to open the mysteries of life, cognizance, and the inter-connected frameworks that support our planet. The boondocks of information continually grow, uncovering new inquiries and difficulties that move researchers into neglected scholarly scenes.

Geological Outskirts: From Posts to Pinnacles:

Topographical investigation has been instrumental in pushing the limits of human comprehension and growing our insight into the World's assorted scenes. The posts, once aloof and puzzling, have become destinations of investigation, with travelers and researchers exploring the frosty regions to concentrate on environ-mental change and figure out the polar biological systems. The investigation of Antarctica, for instance, addresses a victory of human strength and logical interest notwithstanding outrageous circumstances.

Mountain climbers, as well, explore the obscure as they rise transcending tops, each highest point addressing a success of both physical and mental difficulties. Mount Everest, the world's most noteworthy pinnacle, has drawn pilgrims and climbers for quite a long time, testing the constraints of human perseverance and the ability to explore misleading scenes.

The Profundities Beneath: Unwinding Maritime Secrets:

The sea profundities, covering more than 66% of the World's surface, stay quite possibly of the least investigated and grasped outskirts. Marine investigation wanders into the pit, using submarines, remotely worked vehicles (ROVs), and independent submerged vehicles (AUVs) to explore the obscure profundities.

The secrets of the remote ocean, from aqueous vents abounding with extraordi-nary life to strange submerged mountain ranges, spellbind researchers and pilgrims the same.

Investigation of the sea's profundities additionally includes uncovering verifi-able mysteries, as submerged archeologists explore submerged delivers and lowered urban areas. The remote ocean, with its outsider scenes and unseen species, keeps on being a wellspring of interest and logical request, with the possibility to open hints about the beginnings of life on The planet and then some.

The Brain's Boondocks: Exploring the Internal Universe:

The obscure isn't bound to outer scenes alone; it additionally stretches out to the inward universe of the human psyche. The investigation of awareness, brain sci-ence, and neuroscience includes exploring the intricacies of mental cycles, feelings, and the complexities of the cerebrum. Neuroscientists, analysts, and rationalists leave on scholarly excursions to figure out the secrets of human idea and insight.

Thoughtful practices and scrutinizing customs offer one more road for exploring the inward domains, with people investigating the strange regions of their own awareness. Rehearses like care and contemplation give devices to exploring the obscure scenes of the brain, encouraging mindfulness and inward change.

Social Investigation and Anthropological Wildernesses:

Social investigation includes exploring the assorted scenes of human social orders, customs, and lifestyles. Anthropologists and ethnographers adventure into unfamiliar regions, concentrating on distant clans, antiquated civilizations, and contemporary subcultures. The investigation of social variety adds to a more profound comprehension of the human experience, revealing insight into the rich embroidery of convictions, customs, and social designs that mold social orders.

Social trade and culturally diverse exchange act as vessels for exploring the obscure regions of various perspectives. The mixing of societies, worked with by globalization and interconnectedness, sets out open doors for common comprehension and appreciation. Investigating social boondocks includes rising above assumptions, embracing variety, and exploring the intricacies of intercultural experiences.

Mechanical Outskirts: Developments and the Strange Future:

Mechanical development impels mankind into strange regions, changing the manner in which we live, convey, and communicate with the world. The coming of man-made reasoning, nanotechnology, and biotechnology addresses an outskirts where researchers and designers explore the moral, social, and logical ramifications of earth shattering headways.

The strange future, molded by arising advancements, welcomes us to explore the moral contemplations and cultural effects of developments that reclassify the limits of plausibility.

Space investigation, moved by progressions in rocket innovation and space travel, keeps on broadening the wildernesses of human reach. The possibility of interplanetary investigation and the colonization of other divine bodies present difficulties and amazing open doors as humankind explores the unfamiliar domains past Earth.

Mysterious Boondocks and Otherworldly Journeys:

Past the unmistakable scenes and logical boondocks, there exist enchanted and otherworldly outskirts that coax searchers on journeys for greatness and illumination. Across societies and from the beginning of time, people have set out on profound excursions, exploring the obscure domains of the spirit, cognizance, and the heavenly.

Enchanted encounters, whether through reflection, supplication, or adjusted conditions of cognizance, offer looks into strange regions that rise above the limits of the material world. The investigation of enchanted wildernesses includes a journey for significance, reason, and association with an option that could be more significant than oneself.

Confronting the Difficulties of the Unexplored world:

Exploring the obscure isn't without its difficulties. The vulnerability, gambles, and intrinsic intricacies of unknown domains request strength, versatility, and a feeling of investigation. Whether confronting the cruel states of polar undertakings, the capricious powers of the remote ocean, or the scholarly difficulties of logical request, pilgrims should face and defeat hindrances on their excursions.

In the domain of the psyche, confronting the obscure includes exploring the complexities of human feelings, defying individual apprehensions, and embracing the vulnerabilities of self-disclosure. Social investigation requires a receptiveness to understanding viewpoints that might vary from one's own, cultivating sympathy and spanning social partitions.

The Job of Interest and Creative mind:

At the core of exploring the obscure falsehoods the main impetus of human interest and creative mind. Interest pushes pioneers to clarify some things, look for replies, and leave on ventures into unfamiliar domains. Creative mind, the capacity to imagine potential outcomes past the known, powers the imaginative soul that drives logical disclosure, creative articulation, and mechanical development.

The tales of pioneers, researchers, and visionaries frequently start with a flash of interest and a readiness to envision a world past the recognizable. From the trail-blazers of room investigation to the writers who investigate the scenes of feeling, the transaction among interest and creative mind shapes the direction of human investigation and disclosure.

Moral Contemplations in Route:

As we explore the obscure, moral contemplations come to the very front. The effect of investigation, whether physical, scholarly, or social, brings up issues about natural supportability, civil rights, and dependable commitment. The safeguarding of neglected biological systems, the moral treatment of native networks, and the dependable utilization of arising advancements are basic contemplations in the route of unknown domains.

Moral investigation likewise reaches out to the domains of logical request, with a guarantee to straightforwardness, respectability, and the mindful utilization of information. As we dig into the secrets of the psyche, social scenes, and innovative wildernesses, moral route includes a principled methodology that considers the prosperity of people, social orders, and the planet.

The Innate Interest of the Unexplored world: Embracing the Secrets Past

In the proceeded with investigation of strange regions, the intrinsic interest with the obscure continues as a main impetus, impelling humankind into domains where questions dwarf responds to. The appeal of secret, whether tracked down in the universe, the profundities of the sea, or the openings of the human psyche, entices pilgrims, researchers, and scholars to wander past laid out limits.

Embracing Vulnerability as an Impetus for Development:

Exploring the obscure requires an eagerness to embrace vulnerability, remembering it not as a deterrent but rather as an impetus for development and disclosure. The difficulties experienced on ventures into strange domains, be they physical, scholarly, or profound, become open doors for strength, flexibility, and the extension of human capacities. It is through standing up to the obscure that people and social orders frequently track down the impulse for advancement and progress.

The affirmation of vulnerability encourages a mentality of constant realizing, where each experience with the obscure turns into a venturing stone toward more profound comprehension. The flexibility created notwithstanding the obscure turns into a wellspring of solidarity, empowering people to explore the intricacies of existence with a feeling of interest and strength.

Social Appreciation Notwithstanding Variety:

In the domain of social investigation, exploring the obscure includes an appreciation for variety and an affirmation of the lavishness that emerges from the mosaic of human encounters. Pilgrims of social outskirts perceive the significance of regarding and figuring out the one of a kind practices, dialects, and conviction frameworks that shape various social orders.

Social appreciation includes rising above generalizations and assumptions, moving toward new domains with an open heart and brain. By cultivating multifaceted exchange and embracing the variety of human articulation, people add to the production of a worldwide embroidery that praises the interconnectedness of the human experience.

Creative mind as a Door to the Inconspicuous:

Creative mind goes about as a strong door to the inconspicuous domains of probability, driving development, innovativeness, and the investigation of novel thoughts. Visionaries who explore the obscure frequently have a sharp capacity to imagine prospects past the ongoing reality, envisioning answers for difficulties and spearheading new ways.

The innovative ability to imagine the obscure isn't restricted to logical investigation alone yet stretches out to artistic expression, writing, and the domains of speculative fiction. Craftsmen and journalists explore the unfamiliar domains of the creative mind, making stories that transport crowds to fantastical universes and challenge the limits of what is considered conceivable.

Moral Route: Offsetting Progress with Liability:

As mankind dives further into unfamiliar domains, moral contemplations become central. The mindful route of the obscure requires a sensitive harmony among progress and the moral treatment of the conditions, networks, and social orders impacted by investigation.

In logical pursuits, moral route involves a promise to straightforwardness, the mindful utilization of information, and contemplations for the expected cultural effects of revelations. In social investigation, moral commitment includes regard for the independence and nobility of the networks experienced, guaranteeing that the investigation cycle contributes decidedly to shared understanding and joint effort.

The Ceaseless Excursion: From one Skyline to another:

The excursion into the obscure is ceaseless, with every disclosure opening new skylines and uncovering beforehand concealed vistas. The idea of the "obscure" ceaselessly develops, pushing the limits of what is viewed as natural and moving mankind to adjust to the always extending wildernesses of information.

From the perceptible compasses of interstellar space to the minuscule complexities of quantum domains, the strange regions stay as huge and fascinating as anyone might think possible. Essentially, the investigation of human awareness, social subtleties, and the neglected capability of innovation moves us toward skylines yet to be completely gotten a handle on.

Protecting the Marvel of Investigation:

In the midst of the quest for information and the route of the obscure, protecting the marvel that goes with exploration is fundamental. The feeling of wonderment and love for the secrets that persevere on the planet, whether as a far off cosmic system, an unseen species, or the conundrum of human cognizance, improves the human experience.

Protecting the marvel of investigation includes developing a careful familiarity with the excellence tracked down in the obscure and an acknowledgment of the interconnectedness of all that exists. The appreciation for the secrets of the universe, the Earth, and the human experience fills in as a directing light, advising us that, in our quest for information, we are members in a great and unfurling story.

The Aggregate Odyssey: Humankind's Common Mission:

In the aggregate odyssey of humankind, the route of the obscure turns into a common journey that rises above individual undertakings. The combined endeavors of wayfarers, researchers, craftsmen, and masterminds add to a common story that traverses societies, disciplines, and ages. As an animal groups, we are joined by the consistent idea of interest, and our aggregate process into the obscure ties us together in the embroidery of human investigation.

Through the ages, the obscure has stayed a timeless buddy, offering the two difficulties and compensations to the people who set out to wander into its domains. The investigation of the obscure isn't just a journey for answers however a continuous discourse with the secrets that characterize the human condition. A demonstration of the unyielding soul drives us forward, empowering us to explore the obscure with a feeling of miracle, lowliness, and the persevering through conviction that the actual excursion holds the way to opening the significant secrets of presence.

Embracing the Excursion of Investigation:

"Exploring the Unexplored world" exemplifies the quintessence of human investigation and the getting through journey for understanding and disclosure. From the furthest reaches of space to the profundities of the human mind, the excursion into unfamiliar regions is a demonstration of the unyielding soul of interest and the voracious yearn for information.

As we explore the obscure, we are called to embrace the excursion with lowliness, regard, and a feeling of miracle. The difficulties and vulnerabilities that accompany investigation are vital to the course of development, learning, and the advancement of human getting it.

In the amazing woven artwork of human investigation, each excursion into the obscure adds to the aggregate account of our species. It is a story woven with the strings of logical request, social trade, mechanical development, and the immortal mission for otherworldly understanding. As we explore the strange domains that entice us, let us lead of interest, directed by the conviction that the actual excursion is a wellspring of illumination and a demonstration of the endless capability of the human soul.

7.1 Historical perspectives on navigation challenges in the region.

Exploring the Bermuda Triangle: Unwinding Verifiable Points of view on Route Difficulties

The Bermuda Triangle, an approximately characterized district in the western piece of the North Atlantic Sea, has long caught the creative mind of people in general because of reports of baffling vanishings of boats and airplane. While the thought of the Bermuda Triangle as a dangerous and mysterious region has become profoundly imbued in mainstream society, looking at verifiable points of view uncovers a more nuanced comprehension of route difficulties around here. This investigation digs into the verifiable setting of route difficulties inside the Bermuda Triangle, taking into account factors like geology, weather conditions, and innovative restrictions that have added to the locale's persona.

Topographical Elements: The Intermingling of Ocean Courses:

The Bermuda Triangle, generally limited by focuses in Miami, Bermuda, and Puerto Rico, envelops a vigorously voyaged oceanic region. By and large, this district has been a union point for ocean courses interfacing Europe, the Americas, and the Caribbean. The nearness of these courses has prompted a high volume of sea traffic going through the Bermuda Triangle, making a complex and possibly risky navigational climate.

One verifiable test looked by mariners exploring this locale is the presence of the Bay Stream, a strong sea flow beginning in the Bay of Mexico. The Inlet Stream streams toward the north along the eastern shoreline of the US prior to turning toward the east toward Europe. Its quick flows and flighty wandering have presented difficulties for ships, affecting their courses and possibly prompting navigational mistakes.

Early Route and the Period of Investigation:

During the Period of Investigation in the fifteenth to seventeenth hundreds of years, European mariners wandered into the Atlantic Sea looking for new shipping lanes and domains. Navigational instruments of this time were simple contrasted with current norms, with sailors depending on fundamental apparatuses like the astrolabe and quadrant for heavenly route.

The absence of exact diagrams and the dependence on heavenly perceptions made route in the vast sea innately testing. The Bermuda Triangle, with its flighty weather conditions and the shortfall of noticeable tourist spots, introduced an imposing navigational riddle for early voyagers. The restricted comprehension of sea flows, joined with the limitlessness of the Atlantic, added a component of vulnerability to sea ventures.

Navigational Dangers in the Brilliant Time of Robbery:

The authentic period known as the Brilliant Time of Robbery (late seventeenth to mid eighteenth hundreds of years) saw an expansion in sea exercises in the Atlantic, with privateers going after dealer vessels and maritime boats. The Bermuda Triangle, with its essential area along shipping lanes, turned into a focal point for privateer movement. Exploring this area during the Brilliant Period of Robbery presented new risks for mariners, including the danger of assaults by infamous privateers like Blackbeard and Calico Jack.

Privateers frequently took advantage of the misleading states of the Bermuda Triangle to trap clueless vessels. The navigational difficulties of the area, combined with the perils presented by privateers, established a climate of elevated risk for oceanic explorers. Verifiable records from this time report various experiences among privateers and boats exploring the Bermuda Triangle, adding to the locale's standing as a dangerous ocean.

Navigational Instruments and Innovative Headways:

As the Period of Investigation gave way to the Time of Sail, headways in navigational instruments started to work on the precision of ocean travel. The sextant, created in the eighteenth 100 years, permitted sailors to quantify the point between a divine body and the skyline with more noteworthy accuracy, empowering more precise assurance of a boat's scope.

Nonetheless, in spite of mechanical headways, route in the Bermuda Triangle stayed testing. The area's eccentric climate, including abrupt tempests and thick haze, could cloud heavenly bodies, making divine route questionable. The shortfall of dependable diagrams and the innate trouble of pinpointing one's area in the vast sea added to the tireless difficulties looked by mariners.

Secrets of the Bermuda Triangle in the twentieth 100 years:

The twentieth century saw a flood in interest and hypothesis with respect to the Bermuda Triangle, energized by revealed episodes of strange vanishings. While a significant number of these episodes have been exposed or made sense of by traditional factors, for example, climate peculiarities and human blunder, the far and wide consideration added to the impression of the Bermuda Triangle as a zone of otherworldly risk.

In the right on time to mid-twentieth hundred years, mechanical headways in flying additionally changed the difficulties of exploring the Bermuda Triangle. The presentation of radio correspondence and radar worked on the capacity of airplane to explore and speak with ground stations, diminishing the dependence on visual route. Regardless of these headways, the Bermuda Triangle kept on being related with high-profile vanishings, remembering the scandalous Flight 19 occurrence for 1945, where five U.S. Naval force planes vanished during a preparation flight.

Weather conditions and Climatic Inconsistencies:

The Bermuda Triangle is known for its unusual and at times serious weather conditions. The assembly of tropical and subtropical air masses in the locale can prompt the fast advancement of tempests, including typhoons. The danger of unexpected and extraordinary climate occasions has generally represented a huge navigational test for the two boats and airplane.

Storms, with their strong breezes and fierce oceans, make conditions that can overpower vessels and airplane. The recurrence of tropical storms in the Atlantic typhoon season, which runs from June to November, adds a component of hazard for those exploring the Bermuda Triangle during this period. Verifiable records and contemporary records feature the job of outrageous climate occasions in oceanic and flight episodes inside the district.

Electronic Route and Contemporary Difficulties:

In the last 50% of the twentieth hundred years and into the 21st hundred years, electronic route frameworks have become standard hardware for boats and airplane. Worldwide Situating Framework (GPS) innovation, satellite correspondence, and high level radar frameworks have extraordinarily upgraded the accuracy and unwavering quality of route in the Bermuda Triangle.

While these mechanical progressions have moderated a portion of the verifiable difficulties related with exploring the locale, the Bermuda Triangle's persona endures. In spite of the accessibility of cutting edge route devices, the immeasurability of the untamed sea, combined with the potential for unexpected and capricious weather conditions changes, keeps on presenting navigational difficulties. Besides, the locale's verifiable standing adds to a waiting feeling of mindfulness among the people who cross its waters and airspace.

The Human Variable: Blunders and Independent direction:

From the beginning of time, the human variable plays had a vital impact in navigational difficulties inside the Bermuda Triangle. Human mistake, whether as errors, misinterpretations, or unfortunate direction, has been a contributing component to episodes and vanishings. The strain of exploring a locale with an apparent emanation of secret might have likewise impacted the mental condition of mariners and pilots, possibly influencing their dynamic cycles.

The mental effect of the Bermuda Triangle's standing is apparent in records of experienced pilots communicating uneasiness or distress while navigating the district. Such mental variables can add to pressure, interruption, and failures to understand the situation, intensifying the navigational difficulties looked by those exploring the Bermuda Triangle.

Search and Salvage Activities: Answering Occurrences:

The authentic difficulties of exploring the Bermuda Triangle are firmly interlaced with search and salvage activities incited by detailed episodes. The limitlessness of the district, joined with the potential for antagonistic weather patterns, has put forth search and salvage attempts especially testing. By and large, the shortfall of cutting edge correspondence innovation further muddled the convenient reaction to crises.

Search and salvage missions in the Bermuda Triangle have frequently elaborate joint effort between worldwide offices, mirroring the locale's situation as a junction for worldwide oceanic and flying courses. The coordination of endeavors among countries, using progressions in correspondence and reconnaissance innovation, has worked on the productivity of search and salvage activities in the area.

Exposing Fantasies and Cultivating Understanding:

As of late, endeavors to expose fantasies and cultivate a more educated understanding regarding the Bermuda Triangle have built up forward momentum. Logical clarifications for revealed episodes, including the job of regular peculiarities, for example, methane hydrate emissions and submerged land highlights, have been advanced to dissipate ideas of heavenly or extraterrestrial inclusion.

By inspecting authentic episodes inside the Bermuda Triangle from the perspective of present day science, analysts try to demystify the district and separate truth from fiction. Understanding the regular and navigational variables at play in the Bermuda Triangle adds to a more levelheaded and proof put together point of view with respect to the difficulties looked by those exploring its waters and airspace.

Exploring Reality In the midst of Fantasy and Secret:

The verifiable points of view on route difficulties in the Bermuda Triangle uncover a complicated exchange of topographical, meteorological, mechanical, and human elements. While the locale has gained notoriety for secret and interest, a nearer assessment features the substantial difficulties that mariners and pilots have looked since the beginning of time.

From the beginning of oceanic investigation to the cutting edge period of trend setting innovation, the Bermuda Triangle has presented navigational difficulties that, on occasion, have demonstrated dangerous. The intermingling of ocean courses, unusual weather conditions, and the mental effect of its perplexing standing have added to a verifiable story that is as much about human experience for all intents and purposes about the secrets of the ocean.

As innovation proceeds to progress and our comprehension of normal peculiarities develops, the persona of the Bermuda Triangle may step by step respect a more grounded enthusiasm for the navigational difficulties inborn around here. By disentangling the verifiable points of view and inspecting the real factors looked by pilots, we can explore a course that isolates fantasy from the real world, encouraging a more profound comprehension of the intricacies of the Bermuda Triangle and the ocean that has long caught the human creative mind.

7.2 How advancements in technology have affected navigation and safety.

Exploring What's to come: The Effect of Mechanical Progressions on Route and Security

The development of innovation has changed the field of route, generally adjusting how people cross the globe and guaranteeing more secure excursions across oceans, skies, and even into space. From old divine route procedures to the accuracy of current satellite-based frameworks, progressions in innovation have reshaped the scene of route and wellbeing. This investigation digs into the significant effect of innovation on route rehearses, security conventions, and the consistent reconciliation of developments that keep on rethinking our capacity to investigate and travel.

Old Route Procedures: From Stars to Sextants:

The foundations of route follow back to old developments that depended on divine signs for direction. Guides would notice the places of stars, the sun, and other divine bodies to decide their area and course. Polynesians, for example, were capable at utilizing the stars, waves, and the flight examples of birds to explore the tremendous scope of the Pacific Sea.

The improvement of instruments, for example, the astrolabe and quadrant stamped huge progressions during the Period of Investigation. These apparatuses permitted sailors to quantify the points between heavenly bodies and the skyline, giving fundamental information to working out their scope. Be that as it may, these early instruments were restricted in precision and depended vigorously on clear skies and talented pilots.

Reforming Route with the Sextant:

The eighteenth century presentation of the sextant denoted a crucial crossroads in route history. This instrument, which estimated the rakish distance between two noticeable articles, permitted sailors to all the more precisely decide their situation adrift. The sextant, combined with exact timekeeping gadgets like the marine chronometer, altogether upgraded the accuracy of divine route.

The precision given by the sextant assumed a urgent part in oceanic investigation and exchange. It empowered mariners to plot more exact courses, diminishing the gamble of navigational blunders and further developing wellbeing on lengthy sea journeys. The blend of divine route and headways in timekeeping turned into the foundation of sea route until the twentieth hundred years.

The Effect of Radio Route: A Progressive Jump:

The mid twentieth century saw one more jump forward with the coming of radio route frameworks. Radio transmissions communicated from ground-based stations permitted airplane and boats to decide their situation by locating their separation from these stations. The Decca and LORAN (Long Reach Route) frameworks were eminent instances of early radio route advancements.

These frameworks gave a critical improvement in route exactness, particularly during unfavorable weather patterns when divine perceptions were testing. Radio route diminished the dependence on viewable signs and presented another period of more secure and more solid travel, especially in regions where exact route was basic.

Heavenly Route Gives Way to Inertial Route Frameworks:

While divine route stayed a dependable technique, the last 50% of the twentieth century saw the development of inertial route frameworks. These frameworks used accelerometers and gyrators to persistently follow shifts in speed and course, permitting vessels and airplane to decide their situation without outer references.

Inertial route frameworks addressed a takeoff from customary strategies, offering a degree of independence and precision that was phenomenal. These frameworks were especially helpful in circumstances where outer references, like divine bodies or radio transmissions, were inaccessible. The military and aviation ventures embraced inertial route for its dependability and accuracy.

The Worldwide Situating Framework (GPS) Insurgency: Accuracy for All:

The apex of route innovation showed up with the Worldwide Situating Framework (GPS). Sent off by the U.S. Division of Guard during the 1970s, GPS at first filled military needs yet was subsequently made accessible for regular citizen use. Containing an organization of satellites in circle around Earth, GPS permits clients to pinpoint their area with wonderful precision.

The presentation of GPS denoted a change in perspective in route. It gave constant situating data, empowering clients to explore with phenomenal accuracy. From handheld gadgets to vehicles and airplane, GPS turned into a basic piece of regular route, improving security and proficiency across different areas.

Upgraded Wellbeing Through Crash Evasion Frameworks:

Innovative progressions haven't been restricted to deciding area alone; they have additionally essentially improved wellbeing through impact aversion frameworks. In the oceanic business, Programmed ID Framework (AIS) innovation permits vessels to trade data about their personality, position, course, and speed. This sharing of information forestalls crashes and guarantees more secure route in clogged waters.

Also, the aeronautics business has embraced Car accident Evasion Frameworks (TCAS), which use radar information to identify close by airplane and give warnings to pilots to stay away from possible crashes. These frameworks assume an imperative part in guaranteeing the security of air travel, particularly in airspace with high traffic thickness.

E-route: Incorporating Data for More secure Oceans:

The idea of e-route has arisen as a comprehensive way to deal with improve wellbeing and productivity in oceanic route. E-route use computerized innovations to incorporate different wellsprings of data, furnishing sailors with a complete and ongoing comprehension of their working climate. This incorporates electronic diagrams, climate information, traffic data, and other pertinent subtleties.

The point of e-route is to work on the route interaction, diminish the gamble of human blunder, and advance situational mindfulness. Via consistently incorporating information and robotizing routine assignments, e-route adds to more secure and more proficient sea tasks. It addresses a computerized change in oceanic route, lining up with the more extensive pattern of digitalization across ventures.

High level Weather conditions Estimating for More secure Excursions:

Innovative headways have altogether worked on our capacity to foresee and answer atmospheric conditions, adding to more secure route. High level weather conditions anticipating frameworks, fueled by supercomputers and satellite information, furnish sailors and pilots with precise and ideal data about weather conditions.

Admittance to ongoing weather conditions refreshes considers better course arranging, assisting vessels and airplane with keeping away from unsafe circumstances. This proactive way to deal with climate the board has demonstrated instrumental in forestalling climate related occurrences and guaranteeing the security of those exploring through testing air conditions.

Accuracy Landing Frameworks in Flight: Improving Air terminal Security:

In flight, accuracy landing frameworks have been a distinct advantage for air terminal security. Instrument Landing Framework (ILS) and Worldwide Route Satellite Framework (GNSS) approaches empower airplane to make exact and safe arrivals, even in antagonistic weather patterns. These frameworks upgrade perceivability for pilots and give direction all through the plummet and landing stages.

The execution of Classification III Instrument Landing Framework (Feline III ILS) permits airplane to land with incredibly low perceivability, diminishing the probability of flight disturbances because of antagonistic climate. This is especially basic for activities at occupied air terminals and during extreme climate occasions.

Independent Route: Molding the Eventual fate of Movement:

The eventual fate of route is progressively entwined with independent frameworks. In both oceanic and avionics spaces, headways in man-made brainpower, AI, and sensor advancements are preparing for independent route. Independent vessels and airplane can possibly upgrade wellbeing, enhance eco-friendliness, and decrease human mistake.

Automated Flying Vehicles (UAVs) and automated surface vessels are as of now being utilized for different applications, from reconnaissance to freight transport. The combination of independent route frameworks will probably reclassify the scene of movement, with suggestions for both wellbeing and functional effectiveness.

Online protection Difficulties: Shielding Route Frameworks:

As route frameworks become more interconnected and dependent on advanced innovations, the issue of network safety has come to the front. Defending route frameworks from digital dangers is pivotal to guaranteeing the trustworthiness and dependability of these frameworks. Unapproved access, information control, or interruption of route signals present critical dangers to the wellbeing and security of oceanic and avionics activities.

Endeavors to improve online protection in route include carrying out vigorous encryption, secure correspondence conventions, and customary framework refreshes. As innovation keeps on propelling, the flexibility of route frameworks against digital dangers will be a basic thought for guaranteeing the wellbeing and security of worldwide travel.

Determination: Exploring an Innovative Outskirts:

The excursion of route from old heavenly perceptions to the accuracy of satellite-based frameworks is a demonstration of human inventiveness and the extraordinary force of innovation. Progressions in route have made travel more secure as well as extended the outskirts of investigation and availability.

The mix of GPS, e-route, independent frameworks, and high level security advancements addresses another period in route. As we explore this mechanical outskirts, it is crucial for address difficulties like network protection and guarantee that the advantages of advancement are offset with powerful security measures.

The continuous development of route innovation holds the commitment of more secure, more productive, and manageable travel. From the immensity of the untamed oceans to the levels of the sky, innovation keeps on forming the manner in which we explore, opening up additional opportunities and guaranteeing that the excursion stays as wonderful as the actual objections. As we explore this consistently evolving scene, the skyline of conceivable outcomes keeps on growing, welcoming us to investigate, find, and embrace the eventual fate of protected and consistent travel.

Chapter 8

The Human Element

The Human Component in Route and Investigation: Exploring the Oceans of Involvement

In the mind boggling embroidery of route and investigation, the human component winds around an account of boldness, interest, and flexibility. From the beginning of marine and divine route to the state of the art innovation of the present space investigation, the job of people in the mission for disclosure is obvious. This investigation digs into the complex components of the human component, looking at its effect on route, the mental parts of investigation, and the harmonious connection between human instinct and mechanical progressions.

The Early Pilots: Spearheading the Oceans with Ability and Instinct:

Some time before the coming of complex route instruments, early travelers depended on a mix of expertise, instinct, and observational ability to cross the immensity of the seas. The Polynesians, for example, explored the Pacific Sea utilizing the stars, sea flows, and the flight examples of birds. Their profound comprehension of the regular world and sharp instinct permitted them to explore with exceptional accuracy across apparently vast scopes of water.

Likewise, during the Time of Investigation, sailors wandered into unknown waters equipped with minimal more than compasses, astrolabes, and graphs. The progress of these early guides relied on their capacity to decipher normal signs, adjust to evolving conditions, and explore by the stars. The human component, as experience and instinct, assumed a focal part in the achievement or disappointment of these oceanic excursions.

Divine Route and the Human Association with the Universe:

Divine route, rehearsed for a really long time, represents the significant association between the human component and the universe. Guides would utilize the places of divine bodies like the sun, moon, and stars to decide their area and course.

This technique required a profound comprehension of cosmology and a private association with the divine circle.

The human component in divine route reached out past simple computations; it included an appreciation for the vast dance of heavenly bodies and a capacity to blend with the rhythms of the universe. Guides became divine choreographers, plotting their courses by lining up with the heavenly groups of stars. This mind boggling dance among mankind and the universe is a demonstration of the well established association between the human soul and the secrets of the universe.

The Brain research of Investigation: Interest, Chance, and the Unexplored world:

At the center of investigation lies the complex transaction of human brain science. The inborn human interest, the longing to unwind secrets, and the readiness to defy the obscure have been main thrusts since forever ago. Pioneers eagerly left on dangerous excursions, driven by a voracious hunger for information and the appeal of disclosure.

The brain research of investigation includes a fragile harmony between the excitement of disclosure and the inborn dangers of wandering into unknown regions. The human component comes to the front as pioneers wrestle with dread, vulnerability, and the mental cost of disconnection during long excursions. The mental strength of travelers turns into a basic calculate their capacity to explore the actual difficulties as well as the psychological and close to home requests of investigation.

The Sentimentalism of Investigation: Workmanship, Writing, and the Human Soul:

Investigation has long caught the creative mind of specialists and essayists, adding to the sentimentalism related with the journey for the unexplored world. Crafted by voyagers, writers, and painters have formed the aggregate impression of investigation, depicting it as a respectable pursuit that rises above the limits of the known.

Writing, specifically, plays had a critical impact in romanticizing investigation. The works of Jules Verne, for instance, filled the public's interest with fantastical excursions to the focal point of the Earth, under the ocean, and past the skies. These stories engaged as well as roused ages to fantasy about investigating the strange domains of the world.

Workmanship, as well, has portrayed the human soul's victory over the difficulties of investigation. Compositions depicting sailors overcoming blustery oceans, space travelers wandering into space, or mountain climbers vanquishing transcending tops summon a feeling of wonderment and deference for the unstoppable human will.

Mechanical Progressions and the Changing Job of People:

The advancement of route apparatuses and advancements has changed the elements of investigation, reshaping the job of people simultaneously. While early pilots depended on manual instruments and heavenly perceptions, the appearance of apparatuses like the sextant, chronometer, and later, GPS, smoothed out the course of route.

Mechanical headways, especially in the twentieth and 21st hundreds of years, have brought robotization and man-made brainpower into route frameworks. Airplane, boats, and space apparatus are presently furnished with refined autopilot frameworks and route programming that can work out courses, adapt to atmospheric conditions, and even land or moor independently. The job of people has moved from manual control to regulating, checking, and pursuing basic choices.

Human Instinct versus Computerized reasoning: Finding Some kind of harmony:

As innovation keeps on propelling, the inquiry emerges: What is the job of human instinct in a period overwhelmed by man-made brainpower? While calculations and AI can handle tremendous measures of information and upgrade courses, the human component stays indispensable in specific parts of route.

Human instinct envelops a profound comprehension of the climate, the capacity to expect surprising difficulties, and the ability to settle on choices in view of experiential information. In situations where unforeseen factors become possibly the most important factor, human instinct turns into a significant resource, supplementing the capacities of innovation.

Finding some kind of harmony between mechanical accuracy and human instinct is critical for guaranteeing protected and powerful route. The cooperative energy between man-made consciousness and the human component fits the qualities of both, making a route framework that isn't simply effective yet in addition versatile to the intricacies of this present reality.

Social Viewpoints on Route: Native Insight and Current Joint effort:

Various societies all over the planet have remarkable viewpoints on route, frequently established in native insight that has been gone down through ages. Native people groups, for example, the Inuit and Maori, created refined navigational procedures in light of their personal information on neighborhood scenes, divine prompts, and normal peculiarities.

As of late, there has been a developing acknowledgment of the worth of native information in route and ecological stewardship. Current route is progressively consolidating conventional works on, cultivating coordinated effort between native pilots and contemporary researchers. This interdisciplinary methodology perceives the rich woven artwork of human insight and tries to gain according to assorted social viewpoints.

The Human Component in Space Investigation: Space explorers as Trailblazers:

The investigation of room acquaints a totally new aspect with the human component. Space explorers, the trailblazers of room investigation, encapsulate the boldness, versatility, and flexibility expected to explore the immeasurability of the universe. Past the specialized mastery, space explorers go through thorough mental preparation to get ready for the seclusion, control, and the interesting difficulties of room travel.

The mental elements of room investigation feature the significance of the human component in keeping up with mental prosperity during expanded missions. The confinement of room, combined with the dazzling perspectives on Earth from space, summons a significant feeling of contemplation and a change in context. Space travelers, as agents of mankind in space, carry the human component to the very front of interstellar investigation.

The Difficulties of Human Spaceflight: From Microgravity to Confinement:

Human spaceflight presents various difficulties that go past the specialized parts of route. Microgravity, the shortfall of regular climatic signs, and the imprisonment of space apparatus present exceptional physiological and mental difficulties to space explorers. The human body goes through transformations in space, influencing bone thickness, bulk, and cardiovascular wellbeing.

The mental difficulties of segregation and the requirement for independence in space feature the strength of the human soul. Space explorers go through broad preparation in group elements, stress the executives, and critical thinking to explore the intricacies of long-span space missions. The human component turns into a significant figure guaranteeing the achievement and prosperity of room voyagers.

The Moral Elements of Investigation: Adjusting Progress and Protection:

As mankind pushes the limits of investigation, moral contemplations come to the very front. The effect of investigation on the climate, biological systems, and native societies brings up issues about dependable route and stewardship. The human component reaches out past the demonstration of exploring to include moral dynamic that offsets progress with the safeguarding of the normal world.

Travelers and pilots convey an obligation to limit their environmental impression, regard nearby societies, and add to reasonable practices. This moral element of investigation underscores the interconnectedness of mankind with the Earth and the significance of shielding the conditions through which we explore.

The Fate of Human Investigation: Towards New Wildernesses:

Looking forward, the fate of human investigation holds the commitment of wandering into new outskirts, both on The planet and then some. From the investigation of the remote ocean to missions to Mars, the human component will keep on molding the course of investigation. Progresses in drive frameworks, life support advances, and man-made reasoning will additionally rethink the opportunities for human space travel.

The combination of human creativity, mechanical development, and a profound regard for the obscure will move mankind towards new skylines. As we explore the unfamiliar regions of room, dive into the secrets of the remote ocean, and investigate immaculate scenes on The planet, the human component will stay the directing power, controlling the course of our aggregate process.

Exploring the Oceans of Involvement:

In the fabulous woven artwork of route and investigation, the human component arises as the string that ties the past, present, and future. From the early pilots who cruised by the stars to the space travelers graphing flows through the universe, the human soul has been the compass directing mankind through the oceans of involvement.

The transaction between human instinct, experience, and mechanical development makes a unique cooperative energy that drives us into new domains of revelation. As we explore the complex waters of the Earth and adventure into the tremendousness of room, the human component stays in charge, guiding the course with interest, boldness, and a constant craving to investigate the unexplored world.

In the continuous story of route and investigation, the human component isn't simply a member; it is the narrator, winding around stories of wins, challenges, and the getting through soul of investigation. As we explore towards the future, the oceans of involvement loosen up before us, welcoming us to leave on new excursions, embrace the obscure, and proceed with the immortal experience of investigation that characterizes the actual quintessence of being human.

8.1 Examining the role of human error in incidents within the Bermuda Triangle.

Exploring the Secrets: Looking at the Job of Human Mistake in Bermuda Triangle Episodes

The Bermuda Triangle, a locale approximately characterized by focuses in Miami, Bermuda, and Puerto Rico, has caught the public creative mind for quite a long time because of detailed episodes of baffling vanishings of boats and airplane. While different hypotheses and theories encompass this baffling region, a basic assessment uncovers that human blunder assumes a critical part in numerous occurrences credited to the Bermuda Triangle. This investigation dives into explicit cases, breaks down contributing elements, and highlights the significance of understanding the job of human blunder in disentangling the secrets of the Bermuda Triangle.

Verifiable Setting: An Embroidery of Strange Vanishings:

The Bermuda Triangle acquired reputation during the twentieth hundred years as reports of unexplained vanishings started to circle. From Flight 19, a group of U.S. Naval force planes that evaporated in 1945, to the vanishing of the dealer transport SS Marine Sulfur Sovereign in 1963, the locale has been related with a progression of baffling episodes. While the Bermuda Triangle isn't formally acknowledged as a risk zone by sea specialists, its standing as a strange and unsafe region continues in mainstream society.

Flight 19: The Scandalous Disappearing Unit:

One of the most notable occurrences connected to the Bermuda Triangle is the vanishing of Flight 19. On December 5, 1945, five U.S. Naval force Justice fighter planes took off from Post Lauderdale, Florida, for a standard preparation mission.

The unit, drove by experienced pilot Lieutenant Charles Taylor, experienced challenges with route and correspondence. As conditions declined, the airplane in the end ran out of fuel, prompting the vanishing of each of the five planes and 14 team individuals.

Human mistake assumed a critical part in the Flight 19 occurrence. Examinations uncovered that Taylor's route blunders probably drove the group off kilter, making them become perplexed over the untamed ocean. As disarray mounted and fuel dwindled, the pilots confronted a basic circumstance exacerbated by unfortunate weather patterns. The sad result of Flight 19 highlights the outcomes of navigational errors and the intensifying impacts of human blunder in testing circumstances.

SS Marine Sulfur Sovereign: An Oceanic Secret:

The oceanic domain has its portion of Bermuda Triangle secrets, and the vanishing of the SS Marine Sulfur Sovereign is a convincing model. In February 1963, the mass transporter, weighed down with liquid sulfur, left Texas for Virginia yet never showed up at its objective. Regardless of broad inquiry endeavors, no destruction or flotsam and jetsam was found, and the destiny of the vessel stays obscure.

While different hypotheses have been proposed, including the chance of an underlying disappointment because of the freight's destructive nature, human blunder can't be limited. The difficulties related with shipping perilous materials request exact route, adherence to somewhere safe conventions, and cautious observing of vessel conditions. A disappointment in any of these viewpoints, perhaps intensified by unfriendly weather patterns, could add to occurrences, for example, the vanishing of the SS Marine Sulfur Sovereign.

Navigational Difficulties and Climate Elements:

The Bermuda Triangle, known for its erratic weather conditions, gives pilots an interesting arrangement of difficulties. Abrupt and serious weather conditions changes, including the quick improvement of tempests, can surprise vessels and airplane. In situations where pilots neglect to expect or answer really to these climate elements, the gamble of occurrences increments fundamentally.

Human mistake in evaluating and adjusting to changing weather patterns has been embroiled in a few Bermuda Triangle episodes. Guides might experience startling tempests, choppiness, or unfriendly ocean conditions, testing their capacity to go with ideal choices and change course appropriately. Inability to explore securely through such weather conditions difficulties can prompt mishaps and add to the general persona encompassing the Bermuda Triangle.

Correspondence Breakdowns and Search and Salvage Difficulties:

Compelling correspondence is principal in guaranteeing the security of vessels and airplane exploring the Bermuda Triangle. Episodes inside this locale frequently include correspondence breakdowns, preventing the convenient reaction of search and salvage groups. In crises, fast and exact correspondence is fundamental for planning salvage endeavors, yet the tremendousness of the Bermuda Triangle presents difficulties to keeping in touch.

Human blunder in correspondence can come from different elements, including specialized breakdowns, confusion of signs, or lacking preparation. Without even a trace of clear correspondence, search and safeguard tasks become really testing, possibly deferring reaction times and lessening the probability of fruitful results. Looking at the job of correspondence breakdowns gives bits of knowledge into the functional difficulties looked by those answering episodes in the Bermuda Triangle.

Mental Variables: Exploring the Puzzler of Dread and Nervousness:

The Bermuda Triangle's persona stretches out past actual difficulties to include mental elements that guides might wrestle with while navigating the district. The air of secret and the standing of the Bermuda Triangle as a hazardous region can add to uplifted degrees of dread and tension among mariners and pilots.

Mental elements might enhance human blunder by impacting dynamic cycles. Guides encountering dread or tension might show hindered judgment, increased feelings of anxiety, or a hesitance to make vital moves. The mental effect of the Bermuda Triangle's standing highlights the significance of understanding the human component in exploring districts with an apparent quality of secret.

Contextual analyses: Examining Explicit Occurrences:

Inspecting explicit episodes inside the Bermuda Triangle gives significant experiences into the interchange of human mistake and natural difficulties. The vanishing of the USS Cyclops in 1918, the Flight 19 episode in 1945, and the evaporating of the freight transport SS El Faro in 2015 deal nuanced viewpoints on the intricacies guides face around here.

USS Cyclops (AC-4):

The USS Cyclops, a U.S. Naval force collier transport, disappeared without a follow in the Bermuda Triangle during The Second Great War. The boat, conveying a full heap of manganese metal, was on a journey from Brazil to Baltimore. In spite of broad hunt endeavors, no destruction or garbage was at any point found. The occurrence stays quite possibly of the best secret in maritime history.

Human blunder is among the contemplations in the USS Cyclops vanishing. The boat was known for solidness issues, and over-burdening might have exacerbated these issues. Also, the group's naiveté with the vessel's taking care of attributes might have added to navigational blunders. The mix of mechanical difficulties and potential human mistake makes a mind boggling story encompassing the USS Cyclops episode.

SS El Faro:

In 2015, the freight transport SS El Faro experienced Tropical storm Joaquin while on the way from Jacksonville, Florida, to San Juan, Puerto Rico. Unfortunately, the boat sank with the deficiency of every one of the 33 group individuals. Examinations uncovered a progression of contributing variables, including the commander's choice to cruise into the way of the storm and the vessel's obsolete wellbeing measures.

Human mistake assumed a huge part in the SS El Faro misfortune. The commander's choice to explore toward the typhoon's increasing way, joined with insufficient gamble appraisal and correspondence breakdowns, added to the vessel's portentous experience with the tempest. The occurrence features the significance of cool headed direction, risk the executives, and correspondence notwithstanding antagonistic weather patterns.

Alleviating Human Mistake: Illustrations for Pilots:

Understanding the job of human mistake in Bermuda Triangle episodes gives significant illustrations to guides confronting comparative difficulties. Relieving the gamble of human mistake includes a blend of preparing, mechanical headways, and a proactive way to deal with security.

Preparing and Training:

Guaranteeing guides are thoroughly prepared and prepared to deal with the interesting difficulties of the Bermuda Triangle is fundamental. Preparing projects ought to incorporate navigational abilities, atmospheric condition acknowledgment, emergency the board, and viable correspondence techniques. Stressing the mental parts of exploring secretive districts can likewise upgrade the flexibility of pilots confronting the unexplored world.

Mechanical Headways:

Utilizing state of the art innovation can improve route security in the Bermuda Triangle. High level weather conditions checking frameworks, ongoing specialized devices, and cutting edge route hardware add to more educated navigation. Independent frameworks and computerized reasoning, when coordinated mindfully, can enhance human capacities and lessen the gamble of navigational mistakes.

Correspondence Conventions:

Laying out vigorous correspondence conventions is pivotal for answering crises in the Bermuda Triangle. Further developing correspondence framework, carrying out excess frameworks, and directing customary drills for crisis situations can upgrade the adequacy of search and salvage tasks. Stressing the significance of clear correspondence in navigational preparation projects can likewise moderate the effect of correspondence breakdowns.

Risk Evaluation and Independent direction:

Pilots should focus on exhaustive gamble appraisals and cool headed dynamic cycles. This incorporates assessing weather conditions estimates, taking into account vessel capacities, and, while relevant, keeping away from known dangerous circumstances. Direction ought to be educated by a mix regarding specialized mastery, experience, and a proactive way to deal with security.

Exploring the Human Element of Secret:

As the Bermuda Triangle keeps on charming the creative mind with its air of secret, a cautious assessment uncovers that human blunder is a critical consider many revealed occurrences. Guides, whether mariners or pilots, work in a dynamic and testing climate where exact navigation, viable correspondence, and versatility are fundamental.

From verifiable vanishings to contemporary misfortunes, figuring out the interaction of human mistake, natural difficulties, and mental elements gives a nuanced viewpoint on the secrets related with the Bermuda Triangle. By gaining from explicit occurrences, carrying out relief procedures, and focusing on preparing and schooling, pilots can explore this baffling district with a more noteworthy consciousness of the likely dangers and difficulties they might experience.

The Bermuda Triangle stays an image of the obscure, welcoming pilots to investigate its waters with wariness, readiness, and an appreciation for the intricacies that lie underneath the surface. As we disentangle the secrets of this locale, the human aspect arises as a vital consider exploring the oceans as well as the domains of interest, investigation, and the persevering through journey for grasping the baffling powers that shape our reality.

8.2 Stories of survival and lessons learned from those who've encountered its mysteries.

Exploring the Puzzler: Accounts of Endurance and Examples Gained from the Bermuda Triangle

The Bermuda Triangle, a district covered in secret and hypothesis, has been the stage for various accounts of endurance despite everything. From unexplained vanishings to frightening experiences with flighty climate, people who have navigated this baffling region share stories of flexibility, cleverness, and the illustrations learned in the midst of the secrets of the Bermuda Triangle. This investigation digs into firsthand records of endurance, inspects the ongoing ideas woven through these stories, and draws bits of knowledge that offer a more profound comprehension of the difficulties presented by this scandalous locale.

Getting through the Components: Stories of Sailors and Pilots:

The Bermuda Triangle's standing for unexpected and serious weather conditions changes has prompted stories of endurance against the powers of nature. Accounts of sailors and pilots exploring through unforeseen tempests, tempestuous oceans, and unfriendly air conditions feature the strength of the individuals who have conquered the secrets of this district.

The Mary Celeste:

The tale of the Mary Celeste, frequently connected to the Bermuda Triangle, is quite possibly of the most getting through sea secret. In 1872, the boat was found unfastened in the Atlantic Sea with no team ready. While the destiny of the team stays obscure, hypotheses recommend that a blend of regular elements, like unpleasant climate and navigational difficulties, may have prompted their choice to leave transport.

The endurance part of the Mary Celeste secret lies in the actual vessel, which kept on floating helpless before the ocean. While the team's destiny stays a secret, the unwanted boat turned into an image of the difficulties looked by sailors in the erratic waters of the Bermuda Triangle.

The Trip of Bruce Gernon:

Bruce Gernon, an accomplished pilot, experienced a strange peculiarity while flying through the Bermuda Triangle in 1970. As he explored through a passage like cloud development, Gernon experienced time peculiarities, electronic breakdowns, and an extraordinary decrease in fuel utilization. In spite of the dreamlike experience, Gernon figured out how to land securely, and his record of the excursion has turned into an eminent story of endurance in the midst of the unexplained.

Gernon's endurance can be credited to his speedy reasoning and capacity to adjust to the unusual conditions. His story stresses the significance of pilot insight, dynamic under coercion, and keeping up with control despite unforeseen difficulties.

The USS Cyclops: A Maritime Secret:

The USS Cyclops, a U.S. Naval force collier transport, evaporated without a follow in the Bermuda Triangle during The Second Great War. The boat's vanishing, quite possibly of the best maritime secret, involved 309 group individuals and stays perplexing right up 'til now. While the destiny of the team stays obscure, the narrative of the USS Cyclops fills in as a frightful sign of the difficulties looked by maritime vessels in the tremendous territory of the Bermuda Triangle.

The endurance viewpoint in this story lies in the getting through secret that encompasses the USS Cyclops. In spite of broad pursuit endeavors, no destruction or garbage has been found, leaving the story unconditional and adding to the persona of the Bermuda Triangle.

Illustrations from Endurance Accounts: Flexibility and Independent direction:

Normal topics rise out of accounts of endurance in the Bermuda Triangle, offering important examples for guides and explorers the same. Versatility to evolving conditions, fast direction, and the capacity to resist the urge to panic under tension are repeating components that add to effective results despite difficulty.

Survivors frequently relate the significance of remaining on track, depending on preparing and experience, and pursuing informed choices in view of the accessible data. The capacity to adjust plans progressively, explore through startling difficulties, and really speak with others demonstrates pivotal in exploring the vulnerabilities of the Bermuda Triangle.

Exploring Mental Difficulties: The Human Component of Endurance:

Past the actual difficulties presented by the Bermuda Triangle, accounts of endurance likewise shed light on the mental angles looked by the people who cross this baffling locale. Segregation, the heaviness of the obscure, and the mental effect of the Bermuda Triangle's standing add to the psychological difficulties experienced by mariners and pilots.

The Andrea Doria and the Stockholm:

In 1956, the Italian sea liner Andrea Doria crashed into the Swedish traveler transport Stockholm off the shore of Nantucket, a region frequently connected with the Bermuda Triangle. The effect brought about the sinking of the Andrea Doria. The survivors confronted not just the actual difficulties of clearing and salvage yet additionally the mental injury of the trial.

The endurance stories of those on board the Andrea Doria and the Stockholm feature the mental flexibility expected to persevere through the consequence of a sea calamity. The experience of confronting mortality, seeing the deficiency of individual travelers, and the vulnerability of salvage all add to the mental cost of such occurrences.

The Trip of John Charles Tighe:

In 1970, John Charles Tighe, a pilot, experienced motor difficulty while flying over the Bermuda Triangle. Compelled to make a crisis arrival adrift, Tighe and his travelers went through days loose on a daily existence pontoon prior to being saved. The mental difficulties of confronting the immensity of the vast ocean, vulnerability about salvage, and the potential for openness and lack of hydration tried the psychological determination of those on board.

Tighe's endurance story highlights the significance of mental strength even with broadened times of vulnerability. The capacity to keep up with trust, support each other, and remain fixed on endurance undertakings becomes vital in exploring the mental difficulties presented by the Bermuda Triangle.

Endurance and Enchantment: Social Viewpoints:

Accounts of endurance in the Bermuda Triangle additionally converge with social viewpoints and enchantment. A few stories incorporate components of unexplained peculiarities, secretive lights, or experiences with the unexplored world. While these angles add layers to the accounts, they likewise add to the more extensive persona related with the Bermuda Triangle.

The Ellen Austin and the Mary Celeste Association:

The Ellen Austin, a yacht, purportedly experienced the Mary Celeste, the scandalous deserted transport, while cruising through the Bermuda Triangle. As indicated by the story, the group of the Ellen Austin chose to tow the Mary Celeste to port, yet the boats became isolated during a tempest. At the point when the Ellen Austin showed up at its objective, the Mary Celeste was by and by missing.

The association between these two sea secrets adds a component of otherworldliness to the endurance accounts. The unexplained vanishing of the Mary Celeste, interweaved with the Ellen Austin's record, features the getting through puzzle of the Bermuda Triangle.

The Legend of the Bermuda Triangle:

The Bermuda Triangle's persona has become profoundly imbued in mainstream society, with accounts of unexplained peculiarities, vanishings, and experiences adding to its unbelievable status. While numerous endurance stories are grounded in substantial encounters and difficulties, the social account encompassing the Bermuda Triangle frequently winds around components of magic, starting the creative mind of the people who try to grasp its secrets.

Survivors who share their encounters become piece of the more extensive story, adding to the developing legend of the Bermuda Triangle. Their firsthand records give looks into the intricacies of exploring a locale where the line among the real world and fantasy frequently obscures.

Past Endurance: Exploring the Profundities of Involvement with the Bermuda Triangle

The narratives of endurance in the Bermuda Triangle tell stories of beating actual difficulties as well as give a focal point through which to investigate the more profound elements of human experience. As we dive further into the accounts of the people who have experienced the secrets of this perplexing district, extra layers of knowledge arise — examples learned, flexibility tried, and the persevering through influence on the people who explored through the unexplored world. This investigation reaches out past the prompt endurance perspectives to dig into the mental fallout, social reverberation, and the continuous mission for grasping the secrets that persevere in the Bermuda Triangle.

Mental Outcome: The Buildup of the Unexplored world:

Overcomers of Bermuda Triangle occurrences frequently wrestle with the waiting mental impacts of their encounters. The feeling of weakness, the showdown with the obscure, and the frequently dreamlike nature of the occasions add to an enduring engraving on the survivors' brains. Understanding the mental fallout offers a nuanced viewpoint on the cost that exploring the Bermuda Triangle can take on the human mind.

The Phantom Boat Peculiarity:

In the old stories of the Bermuda Triangle, stories of phantom boats — vessels that apparently disappear just to return or float without a team — add a component of mystery to the mental outcome of endurance. The individuals who have seen or experienced experiences with phantom boats discuss the enduring effect on their view of the real world. The obscured lines between the substantial and the illogical add to a feeling of disquiet that waits long after the prompt danger has passed.

The mental buildup of experiencing phantom boats adds a layer of intricacy to the survivor experience. The exchange between the known and the obscure encourages a feeling of vagueness that shapes the survivors' view of their own stories, prompting a proceeding with journey for importance and understanding.

Post-Horrible Pressure and Ways of dealing with stress:

Past the otherworldly, the difficulties presented by navigational crises in the Bermuda Triangle can set off post-awful pressure among survivors. The unexpected and dangerous nature of these occurrences can leave an enduring effect on psychological wellness. Methods for dealing with especially difficult times, both individual and group, become significant in exploring the mental fallout of endurance.

A few survivors find comfort in sharing their encounters, either through narrating, support gatherings, or restorative mediations. Others might foster survival techniques established in a reestablished appreciation forever, a developed association with otherworldliness, or a guarantee to bringing issues to light about the difficulties of exploring the Bermuda Triangle. Understanding the assorted manners by which survivors adapt reveals insight into the intricacy of the human reaction to horrendous accidents.

Social Reverberation: Stories that Rise above Existence:

The tales of endurance in the Bermuda Triangle resound with the people straightforwardly involved as well as inside the more extensive social setting. These stories become piece of the shared awareness, adding to the developing folklore and interest encompassing the Bermuda Triangle. As these accounts rise above reality, they mesh themselves into the texture of social stories, impacting how social orders see the secrets of this scandalous locale.

Writing, Film, and Mainstream society:

The Bermuda Triangle has been a wellspring of motivation for writing, film, and mainstream society. From exemplary works of fiction to blockbuster motion pictures, the accounts of endurance become stories that catch the creative mind of crowds around the world. The social reverberation of these accounts stretches out past genuine records, molding how the Bermuda Triangle is depicted and seen in the more extensive public awareness.

Survivors who decide to share their encounters add to the social story encompassing the Bermuda Triangle. Their accounts become strings in the embroidered artwork of secret and interest that has powered endless works of fiction and genuine, sustaining the appeal of the unexplored world.

The travel industry and Sea Investigation:

The social effect of Bermuda Triangle stories stretches out to the travel industry and oceanic investigation. The district's standing as a puzzling and possibly hazardous region draws in inquisitive swashbucklers trying to disentangle its mysteries. Visits, narratives, and endeavors based on the Bermuda Triangle draw upon the genuine accounts of endurance to connect with crowds and sustain the persona of the locale.

Survivors who become advocates for dependable investigation and mindfulness add to molding the social story encompassing the Bermuda Triangle. Their firsthand records, frequently shared through open gatherings or cooperative undertakings, offer a grounded viewpoint that differentiations with sensationalized depictions in well known media.

The Continuous Journey for Grasping: From Survivors to Agents:

Overcomers of Bermuda Triangle episodes frequently become incidental examiners, driven by a significant craving to comprehend the secrets they have experienced. The journey for answers reaches out past private endurance to a more extensive investigation of the variables that add to the locale's baffling standing. As survivors share their accounts, they contribute significant experiences that illuminate progressing examination and fuel the aggregate mission for understanding.

Logical Request and Investigation:

The secrets of the Bermuda Triangle have provoked logical request and investigation pointed toward demystifying the district. Survivors who effectively draw in with logical examinations contribute firsthand viewpoints that illuminate research endeavors. Coordinated efforts between researchers, sea specialists, and survivors give a complex way to deal with understanding the natural, navigational, and environmental variables at play in the Bermuda Triangle.

The continuous mission for understanding rises above individual encounters, turning into an aggregate undertaking that overcomes any barrier between recounted proof and experimental exploration. Survivors who partake in or support logical request become fundamental supporters of unwinding the intricacies of the Bermuda Triangle.

Promotion and Mindfulness:

A few survivors change from being observers to becoming supporters for mindfulness and capable investigation. Their firsthand information on the difficulties presented by the Bermuda Triangle positions them as voices of expert in conversations about route security, natural elements, and the requirement for informed dynamic in the locale.

Support endeavors drove by survivors add to a culture of security and obligation among pilots. By sharing examples gained from their encounters, survivors assume a vital part in forming the story encompassing the Bermuda Triangle, underscoring the significance of readiness, preparing, and adherence to best practices in route.

Exploring the Embroidered artwork of Involvement:

The tales of endurance in the Bermuda Triangle structure a rich embroidery that reaches out past the quick difficulties of route. They wind around together topics of mental strength, social effect, and the continuous mission for understanding. Survivors, incidentally push into the spotlight of the obscure, become storytellers of encounters that rise above the limits of general setting.

As we explore the profundities of these accounts, we observe that endurance in the Bermuda Triangle isn't simply an actual accomplishment; it is an excursion through the intricacies of human experience. From the mental repercussions to social reverberation and the continuous journey for understanding, survivors add to a story that resounds with interest, challenges predispositions, and welcomes a more profound investigation of the secrets that persevere in the mysterious waters of the Bermuda Triangle.

The narratives of endurance from the Bermuda Triangle structure an embroidery of strength, cleverness, and the persevering through human soul even with the unexplored world. Whether adrift or in the skies, people who have navigated this puzzling area share consistent ideas of versatility, dynamic under tension, and the capacity to stand up to mental difficulties.

Endurance in the Bermuda Triangle isn't simply an actual achievement; it is a demonstration of the human ability to explore the persona of the unexplored world. The examples gained from these stories stretch out past the geological limits of the Bermuda Triangle, offering experiences into the more extensive characteristics of boldness, determination, and the human impulse for endurance.

As we unwind the tales of the individuals who have experienced the secrets of the Bermuda Triangle and arose as survivors, we gain a more profound comprehension of the intricacies that characterize this district. Whether saw from the perspective of sea fiascos, flying peculiarities, or social legends, the accounts of endurance entice us to explore into the great beyond of secret, embracing the significant examples that rise out of the human involvement with the baffling waters of the Bermuda Triangle.

Chapter 9

Beyond Borders

Past Boundaries: Investigating the Interconnected Universe of Globalization

In the contemporary scene, the idea of "Past Lines" encapsulates the extraordinary power of globalization, rising above geological, social, and monetary limits. This extensive peculiarity has reshaped the manner in which social orders associate, economies work, and societies develop. As we dive into the multi-layered components of "Past Boundaries," we uncover a story that includes exchange and trade, social trade, mechanical mix, and the complicated transaction among neighborhood and worldwide elements.

Exchange and Business: A Worldwide Monetary Embroidery:

At the core of "Past Lines" lies the mind boggling woven artwork of worldwide exchange and business. The interconnectedness of economies, worked with by progressions in transportation and correspondence, has made an organization where merchandise, administrations, and capital stream flawlessly across public limits.

The Ascent of Worldwide Inventory Chains:

Globalization has led to complex stockpile chains that range landmasses. From unrefined components to completed items, each phase of creation frequently happens in various corners of the world. This interconnected trap of creation cultivates proficiency, specialization, and cost-viability, driving the driving force of the worldwide economy.

The development of supply chains features the relationship of countries, where disturbances in a single region of the planet can resonate across enterprises and boundaries. The idea of "Past Lines" is typified by the unpredictable dance of products as they navigate the globe, winding around together the fortunes of different economies.

Global Money and Venture:

Past the development of unmistakable products, worldwide money and speculation comprise one more crucial element of the worldwide financial scene. Monetary business sectors work in a borderless domain, with capital streaming across borders continuously. Speculation portfolios are different and interconnected, mirroring a globalized way to deal with abundance creation.

The difficulties and chances of this interconnected monetary world highlight the requirement for cooperative administrative systems, risk the executives, and global participation. The "Past Lines" worldview in finance brings to the very front inquiries of responsibility, straightforwardness, and the common obligation of the worldwide local area.

Social Trade: Crossing over Contrasts and Encouraging Comprehension:

Globalization has introduced a time of exceptional social trade, where thoughts, values, and customs cross lines, advancing the aggregate embroidery of human experience. The intermixing of societies has significant ramifications for personality, variety, and the common accounts that tight spot mankind.

The Globalization of Media and Amusement:

The approach of computerized correspondence has launch media and diversion into a worldwide field. Films, music, writing, and news circle easily, presenting crowds to a heap of viewpoints and stories. The combination of different social impacts has led to a worldwide mainstream society that rises above public limits.

Be that as it may, this social trade isn't without challenges. The gamble of social homogenization, where nearby subtleties are eclipsed by worldwide patterns, prompts inquiries regarding the conservation of social variety. Finding some kind of harmony between social trade and protection turns into a sensitive dance in the "Past Lines" scene.

Language and Correspondence:

In the interconnected world, language fills in as both an extension and an obstruction. The strength of specific dialects in the domains of business, science, and strategy brings up issues of semantic variety and inclusivity. All the while, headways in interpretation advancements work with correspondence across etymological limits, separating customary boundaries.

The development of language in the "Past Boundaries" setting prompts reflections on etymological character, the power elements intrinsic in language use, and the job of correspondence in forming diverse comprehension. As boundaries obscure in the etymological scene, the test is to guarantee that different voices track down reverberation in the worldwide discussion.

Mechanical Reconciliation: The Computerized Outskirts:

Mechanical progressions structure a foundation of the "Past Lines" story, moving humankind into a period where data, development, and network have no limits. The advanced unrest has changed how we live and fill in as well as re-imagined the idea of lines in the domains of information, coordinated effort, and network.

The Web and Data Stream:

The web, an image of the borderless computerized age, fills in as a conductor for the fast spread of data. From web-based entertainment stages to online media sources, the trading of thoughts happens continuously, cultivating a globalized public talk. Notwithstanding, the uncontrolled progression of data additionally raises worries about falsehood, network protection, and the moral elements of advanced correspondence.

The "Past Boundaries" scene in the computerized domain prompts reflections on the obligations of tech monsters, the job of states in directing web-based spaces, and the requirement for a worldwide discussion on computerized morals. Exploring this unfamiliar region requires a sensitive harmony among transparency and protections.

Advancement and Cross-Line Coordinated effort:

Advancement flourishes in a climate where thoughts stream uninhibitedly across borders. The cooperative idea of logical examination, mechanical advancement, and innovative undertakings rises above public limits. Global examination groups, joint endeavors, and cross-line associations impel humankind into new boondocks of information and revelation.

In any case, the cooperative idea of development likewise delivers inquiries of value, access, and the dispersion of advantages. As leap forwards in science and innovation shape the future, the test lies in guaranteeing that the advantages are shared around the world and add to the prosperity of different networks.

Ecological Relationship: Worldwide Difficulties, Worldwide Arrangements:

The ecological difficulties confronting the planet highlight the interconnectedness of countries and the basic for cooperative, cross-line arrangements. Environmental change, biodiversity misfortune, and contamination perceive no lines, requiring a common obligation to supportable practices and natural stewardship.

Transboundary Natural Issues:

Natural corruption frequently rises above political limits, requiring purposeful endeavors on a worldwide scale. From deforestation to transboundary contamination, the environmental effect of human exercises requests a "Past Lines" point of view. Peaceful accords and cooperative drives become urgent in tending to ecological difficulties that influence the prosperity of the whole planet.

The desperation of environment activity places natural worries at the very front of the worldwide plan. The "Past Boundaries" move toward in natural administration mirrors an acknowledgment that the wellbeing of the planet is unpredictably connected to the activities and strategies of countries all over the planet.

Maintainable Turn of events and Worldwide Objectives:

The quest for maintainable improvement requires an aggregate obligation to tending to worldwide difficulties while guaranteeing the prosperity of present and people in the future. The Unified Countries Supportable Improvement Objectives

(SDGs) give a structure to worldwide collaboration, encouraging countries to co-operate to destroy neediness, advance balance, and safeguard the planet.

The "Past Lines" worldview in reasonable improvement provokes countries to move past personal circumstance and think about the more extensive effect of their approaches and activities. As the world looks for a way to a more feasible future, the interconnectedness of countries turns into a main impetus for positive change.

Difficulties and Scrutinizes of Globalization:

While the "Past Boundaries" story proclaims another time of interconnectedness, it isn't without its difficulties and investigates. The lopsided conveyance of advantages, social authority, and the disintegration of neighborhood independence bring up issues about the maintainability and inclusivity of globalization.

Imbalance and Financial Abberations:

Globalization has added to financial development on a worldwide scale, yet its advantages are not disseminated similarly. Variations in pay, admittance to assets, and financial open doors endure, both inside and between countries. The test is to address these disparities and guarantee that the advantages of globalization arrive at underestimated networks.

The "Past Boundaries" viewpoint prompts a reexamination of financial frameworks, exchange strategies, and global collaboration to encourage comprehensive development. Decreasing financial differences turns into a moral and functional basic in the journey for a more impartial worldwide society.

Social Homogenization and Character Disintegration:

As societies blend in the worldwide field, there is a gamble of social homogenization, where prevailing social stories eclipse neighborhood customs. The disintegration of social characters raises worries about the protection of variety and the remarkable articulations of human legacy.

Shielding social variety in the "Past Boundaries" period requires a fragile harmony between worldwide trade and nearby protection. Arrangements that advance social inclusivity, instructive drives, and grassroots endeavors to celebrate social legacy become fundamental in moderating the dangers of character disintegration.

The Future of "Past Boundaries": Exploring Intricacy with Reason:

As we explore the intricacies of the "Past Boundaries" scene, what's to come coaxes with the two difficulties and valuable open doors. The way ahead requires a nuanced comprehension of the interconnected powers molding our reality and a common obligation to building a more comprehensive, manageable, and simply worldwide society.

Worldwide Collaboration and Discretion:

The difficulties of the 21st century request a restored obligation to worldwide collaboration and discretion. Resolving worldwide issues, from general wellbeing emergencies to international pressures, requires cooperative endeavors that rise above public interests. Strategy turns into a fundamental apparatus in exploring the intricacies of the "Past Lines" world.

Multilateral organizations, conciliatory dealings, and discretionary discourse become basic components for cultivating understanding and settling clashes. The basic is to fabricate extensions of participation that work with exchange, cooperation, and the quest for shared objectives.

Worldwide Citizenship and City Commitment:

The idea of worldwide citizenship acquires conspicuousness in the "Past Boundaries" time. People, enabled by innovation and interconnected networks, have the ability to add to worldwide discussions, advocate for change, and participate in urban activities that rise above public limits.

Training assumes a urgent part in supporting worldwide citizenship, cultivating sympathy, and imparting a feeling of obligation toward the prosperity of the planet and its occupants. As people embrace their jobs as worldwide residents, they become specialists of positive change in the journey for an additional equitable and economical world.

Moral Initiative and Corporate Obligation:

Initiative, whether in people in general or confidential area, takes on another aspect in the "Past Lines" setting. Moral administration, grounded in standards of reasonableness, obligation, and manageability, turns into a main impetus for positive change. Corporate elements, perceiving their worldwide effect, embrace social obligation and ecological stewardship as necessary parts of their central goal.

The convergence of business and morals turns into a point of convergence in the "Past Lines" story. From fair work practices to natural protection, pioneers in different areas assume a significant part in molding a worldwide scene that focuses on moral contemplations and capable practices.

Exploring the Interconnected Embroidered artwork of Humankind:

The story of "Past Boundaries" unfurls as a powerful embroidery, woven from the strings of monetary reliance, social trade, innovative combination, and the common difficulties and desires of humankind. In exploring this interconnected scene, the basic is to embrace the intricacy with reason, recognizing the association that ties us together.

The excursion into what's in store requires an aggregate obligation to building scaffolds of grasping, cultivating inclusivity, and tending to the variations that continue in our interconnected world. As we explore the "Past Lines" landscape, the extravagance of variety, the force of cooperation, and the common obligation regarding the prosperity of the planet become core values in forming a more amicable and impartial worldwide society.

9.1 Discussing international perspectives on the Bermuda Triangle.

Exploring the Riddle: Global Points of view on the Bermuda Triangle

The Bermuda Triangle, a locale saturated with secret and sea interest, has caught the minds of individuals all over the planet. Extending from the places of Miami, Bermuda, and Puerto Rico, this cryptic region has been related with a horde of unexplained vanishings of boats and airplane. While the secrets of the Bermuda Triangle have essentially revolved around the North Atlantic Sea, its worldwide reverberation stretches out a long ways past geological lines. Global points of view on the Bermuda Triangle offer a nuanced focal point through which to look at the social, logical, and folkloric understandings that different countries bring to this getting through sea mystery.

Social and Folkloric Viewpoints:

Caribbean Old stories and Mystery:

In the Caribbean, the Bermuda Triangle is much of the time implanted in nearby legends, where stories of apparition ships, puzzling lights, and mystifying peculiarities have been gone down through ages. The district's social extravagance and profound practices interweave with the secrets of the Bermuda Triangle, making an embroidery of stories that mirror the perplexing connection among people and the ocean.

Caribbean societies have long held convictions in otherworldly powers and substances occupying the waters, adding to the persona encompassing the Bermuda Triangle. Neighborhood viewpoints frequently mix verifiable occasions with legendary components, bringing about accounts that rise above the limits between the known and the puzzling.

Latin American Points of view:

Latin American countries arranged around the edges of the Bermuda Triangle, like the Dominican Republic and Cuba, have their own translations of the secrets that unfurl in these waters. Social customs, went down through narrating and old stories, shape the manner in which networks see the Bermuda Triangle and its effect on marine.

In Latin American viewpoints, the Bermuda Triangle is once in a while related with legendary animals or unbelievable stories of lost civic establishments underneath the waves. The mix of native convictions, pilgrim history, and sea fables adds to a rich embroidery of translations that mirrors the different social scenes of the district.

Logical and Navigational Bits of knowledge:

Worldwide Oceanic Coordinated effort:

The Bermuda Triangle, arranged in one of the world's most active transportation paths, has drawn the consideration of global oceanic associations and beach front states. Cooperative endeavors including the US, the Unified Realm, Caribbean countries, and others center around guaranteeing safe route through these waters. The Global Sea Association (IMO) assumes a significant part in advancing navigational security and tending to expected perils in the district.

Logical investigations and navigational examination add to a worldwide comprehension of the ecological variables that might add to occurrences inside the Bermuda Triangle. Worldwide collaboration in sharing information, directing exploration, and executing security estimates highlights the significance of a brought together way to deal with oceanic difficulties.

Russian and European Points of view:

Countries with a stake in the Atlantic Sea, like Russia and European nations, contribute their viewpoints to the continuous talk on the Bermuda Triangle. Logical examinations from these districts frequently center around maritime peculiarities, atmospheric conditions, and topographical elements that might impact route in the North Atlantic.

The European Space Organization (ESA) and Russia's space office, Roscosmos, have participated in satellite-based examinations to screen ecological circumstances in the Bermuda Triangle. These worldwide coordinated efforts bring a multi-disciplinary way to deal with understanding the complicated communications that happen in the district, underlining the requirement for a worldwide viewpoint in disentangling the secrets.

Media and Mainstream society Impact:

Worldwide Media Portrayal:

The Bermuda Triangle's persona reaches out to a worldwide crowd from the perspective of global media. Narratives, movies, and TV programs delivered by networks from different nations add to molding discernments and energizing the interest with the secrets of this area.

The worldwide spread of Bermuda Triangle stories through media channels supports the mystery related with the area. Various societies decipher these stories through their extraordinary points of view, making a mosaic of convictions and translations that resound with crowds all over the planet.

Asian Viewpoints:

In Asia, the Bermuda Triangle has tracked down its place in mainstream society, with different countries adding to the continuous account. Asian news sources frequently investigate the secrets and legends encompassing the Bermuda Triangle, mixing neighborhood narrating customs with the worldwide appeal of the conundrum.

While the locale geologically lies a long way from the Bermuda Triangle, the social effect of its secrets is clear in Asian portrayals of the peculiarity. This reflects how the sea secrets of one region of the planet can catch the aggregate creative mind on a worldwide scale.

Verifiable and Archeological Settings:

Frontier Associations and Authentic Stories:

The verifiable setting of provincial investigation and shipping lanes crosses with the secrets of the Bermuda Triangle. European countries, including Spain, Portugal, and the Assembled Realm, assumed huge parts in molding the sea history of the

Atlantic Sea. The remainders of provincial time boats and ancient rarities in the waters around the Bermuda Triangle add layers to the authentic story.

Worldwide viewpoints on the Bermuda Triangle frequently think about the effect of frontier narratives on route, wrecks, and the potential social impacts that have added to the locale's atmosphere of secret. Verifiable reports, logs, and sea files from various countries offer a different cluster of points of view on the situation that transpired in these waters.

African Oceanic Customs:

African countries with shores lining the Atlantic Sea contribute exceptional points of view established in oceanic practices. The oral chronicles of beach front networks, went down through ages, frequently incorporate references to the secrets of the ocean. From fables about ocean spirits to records of unbelievable journeys, these points of view offer bits of knowledge into how African societies see the sea obscure.

The effect of the transoceanic slave exchange, with its verifiable association with the Atlantic Sea, additionally impacts the manner in which African countries view the secrets of the Bermuda Triangle. The transaction of verifiable stories, social practices, and oceanic legends shapes an unmistakable point of view on this mysterious district.

Navigational Difficulties and Security Concerns:

Asian Sea Courses and Wellbeing Measures:

Asian countries, with their powerful oceanic customs and clamoring shipping lanes, add to the worldwide discussion on navigational difficulties and wellbeing concerns. The South China Ocean, a district crossed by significant transportation paths, has its own arrangement of navigational difficulties, provoking countries in the locale to foster wellbeing conventions and cooperative drives.

Viewpoints from Asian sea specialists frequently draw matches between the difficulties looked in the South China Ocean and those experienced in the Bermuda Triangle. The trading of information and best practices between countries features the interconnected idea of sea security on a worldwide scale.

Center Eastern Points of view:

Countries in the Center East, arranged along crucial sea courses like the Persian Bay and the Red Ocean, draw in with the talk on navigational security. The Suez Trench, a key stream associating the Mediterranean and Red Oceans, underlines the significance of worldwide participation in guaranteeing the smooth progression of sea traffic.

Center Eastern points of view on navigational difficulties frequently draw upon encounters in overseeing in the middle of delivery paths and tending to likely dangers. The examples learned in these areas contribute significant bits of knowledge to the more extensive conversations on oceanic security and the cooperative endeavors expected to explore complex streams.

An Embroidery of Viewpoints Revealed:

The Bermuda Triangle, with its secrets and oceanic legend, rises above topographical limits, bringing worldwide viewpoints into its account. From the Caribbean to Asia, from Russia to Africa, the conundrum of the Bermuda Triangle has woven itself into the social, logical, and folkloric texture of countries all over the planet. As different viewpoints join, an embroidery of understandings arises, mirroring the widespread interest with the obscure and the getting through charm of oceanic secrets.

Global viewpoints on the Bermuda Triangle highlight the interconnected idea of humankind's relationship with the ocean. Whether saw from the perspective of legends, logical request, media portrayal, or navigational security, the secrets of the Bermuda Triangle inspire a common interest that knows no boundaries. As the worldwide local area keeps on exploring the waters of the obscure, the riddle of the Bermuda Triangle stays a demonstration of the getting through force of oceanic stories to catch the aggregate creative mind on a really global scale.

9.2 How different cultures interpret and perceive the enigma.

Investigating Social Points of view on the Puzzler: A Multi-layered Excursion

The idea of the conundrum is a general and immortal peculiarity that has fascinated humankind across societies and ages. A conundrum is something strange, baffling, and hard to comprehend, and its translation frequently shifts fundamentally relying upon social foundations. In this investigation, we dig into the manners in which various societies decipher and see the mystery, analyzing the different focal points through which social orders figure out the baffling and the unexplored world.

1. **Western Viewpoints**

1. **Traditional Greek Way of thinking**

    In traditional Greek way of thinking, the conundrum was in many cases seen as a test to be tackled. Masterminds like Socrates, Plato, and Aristotle moved toward secrets with a reasonable and scientific mentality, looking for consistent clarifications for the apparently baffling. The possibility that information is the way to unwinding riddles turned out to be profoundly imbued in Western thought.

2. **Judeo-Christian Customs**

    In Judeo-Christian customs, the puzzler is frequently connected to divine secrets and the mysterious idea of God. The Holy book, for instance, is loaded with cryptic stories and anecdotes that welcome adherents to consider the authentic secrets. The idea of confidence itself turns into a method for exploring and acknowledge the cryptic parts of life.

3. **Illumination Logic**

During the Illumination, another flood of reasoning arose in Western culture, stressing reason and suspicion. Edification scholars tried to demystify the world through science and reason, testing conventional understandings of riddles. The shift from strict clarifications to logical request denoted a tremendous change in how Western social orders moved toward the unexplored world.

II. Eastern Points of view

1. **Taoism**

   Taoist way of thinking in old China saw the conundrum as a vital piece of the normal request. The Tao Te Ching, a primary text of Taoism, underscores the significance of embracing the secret of presence and streaming with the vast powers. The puzzle isn't something to be tackled yet rather a power to be orchestrated with.

2. **Harmony Buddhism**

   In Harmony Buddhism, the mystery is much of the time utilized as a device for illumination. Koans, incomprehensible proclamations or questions, are utilized to push experts past coherent reasoning and into an immediate encounter of the inexpressible. The puzzler, in this unique situation, turns into a method for rising above standard getting it and taking advantage of a higher cognizance.

3. **Hindu Magic**

Inside Hinduism, particularly in the magical customs like Vedanta and Tantra, the puzzler is viewed as an impression of the heavenly play (Lila) of the universe. The truth is viewed as multi-layered and loaded with oddities, welcoming people to investigate the layers of presence outside customary ability to comprehend. The conundrum, hence, turns into an entryway to profound disclosure.

III. Native Viewpoints

1. **Local American Practices**

   Numerous native societies all over the planet, including Local American practices, have a profound association with the normal world. The conundrum, in these unique circumstances, is much of the time exemplified in the secrets of the land, creatures, and normal cycles. Customs and functions are utilized to draw in with the riddle and look for direction from the otherworldly domain.

2. **African Animism**

In different African societies rehearsing animism, the mystery is entwined with the confidence in spirits possessing the regular world. Ceremonies, moves, and representative practices are utilized to speak with these spirits and explore the strange powers that influence life. The conundrum is embraced as a wellspring of otherworldly interconnectedness.

IV. Contemporary Globalized Points of view

1. Logical Realism

In the contemporary time of logical realism, the mystery is in many cases moved toward from the perspective of experimental request and proof based thinking. Science looks to demystify the obscure, giving clarifications to peculiarities that were once thought to be cryptic. This viewpoint, while fruitful in numerous areas, likewise brings up moral and existential issues about the restrictions of logical reductionism.

2. Postmodern Relativism

Postmodern points of view challenge the idea of a general understanding of the riddle. All things being equal, they feature the emotional and socially developed nature of importance. Various people group and people, as per this view, may build their own accounts and understandings of the riddle in light of their novel social settings and encounters.

V. Center Eastern Points of view

1. Islamic Mystery (Sufism)

In the mysterious custom of Islam, known as Sufism, the riddle is moved toward through otherworldly contemplation and a journey for divine association. Sufi artists and thinkers frequently utilize figurative language to convey the unspeakable idea of the heavenly. The mystery, in this specific situation, addresses the out of reach yet powerful secrets of God, empowering disciples to look for a more profound figuring out through consideration and commitment.

2. Persian Otherworldliness

Drawing from the rich embroidery of Persian magic, exemplified by figures like Rumi and Attar, the puzzle is depicted as an excursion of the spirit. Representative accounts and figurative verse portray the human journey for importance and amazing quality. The puzzle, in Persian magic, turns into a representation for the significant secrets of presence and the spirit's longing for get-together with the heavenly.

VI. Southeast Asian Points of view

1. Buddhism

In different Southeast Asian societies affected by Buddhism, the puzzler is intently attached to the idea of temporariness and the pattern of life, passing, and resurrection (samsara). The tricky idea of the real world and the endless transition of presence are typified in the puzzle, provoking adherents to look for edification and freedom from the cycle through contemplation and moral living.

2. **Animist Practices**

A few native animist customs in Southeast Asia see the mystery through their association with nature spirits and familial powers. Customs and services are performed to pacify and speak with these spirits, exploring the baffling elements of the regular world. The riddle, in this specific situation, is implanted in the texture of day to day existence and public practices.

VII. Cold and Subarctic Native Points of view

1. **Inuit and Yupik Societies**

   In the Cold and Subarctic districts, for example, among the Inuit and Yupik people groups, the riddle takes on one of a kind qualities attached to the unforgiving climate. The huge spreads of ice and snow, combined with the outrageous circumstances, add to a feeling of secret and wonderment. Native information frameworks consolidate accounts, tunes, and customs that address the conundrum of endurance in these difficult scenes.

2. **Shamanic Practices**

Shamanic rehearses inside Icy and Subarctic societies include people who can explore the profound domains and speak with inconspicuous powers. The conundrum is frequently entwined with the shaman's excursion to acquire experiences, mending, and direction. Formal functions, drumming, and daze like states are utilized to get to the confounding aspects past the material world.

VIII. Maritime Viewpoints

1. **Polynesian Route**

   In the tremendous breadths of the Pacific Sea, Polynesian societies created complex route procedures that depended on the puzzling signs of the regular world. Divine bodies, sea flows, and bird relocations filled in as guides for sailors. The mystery, in this specific situation, isn't something to be unraveled yet rather a wellspring of shrewdness that is unpredictably woven into the texture of nautical practices.

2. **Dreamtime in Australian Native Culture**

The Native societies of Australia see the puzzle through the Dreamtime, a profound and cosmological idea. Dreamtime stories and images convey the production of the world and its continuous interconnectedness. The riddle, in this perspective, is a consistently present part of the real world, welcoming people to draw in with the mysterious components of presence through ceremonies, workmanship, and narrating.

IX. South American Points of view

1. **Amazonian Shamanism**

   Inside the different embroidery of Amazonian societies, shamanic rehearses assume a focal part in exploring the mystery. Plant drugs, for example, ayahuasca, are utilized to incite changed conditions of awareness, permitting shamans to speak with spirits and gain bits of knowledge into the secrets of the regular world. The puzzler, in Amazonian shamanism, is a dynamic and living power that requires steady commitment and respect.

2. **Incan Cosmology**

The Inca progress in South America had a perplexing cosmology that coordinated the mystery into how its might interpret the universe. The strange domains of the sky, earth, and hidden world were interconnected through customs and services. The conundrum, in Incan culture, was a consecrated part of life, and the arrangement of divine occasions held significant profound importance.

X. Globalized Metropolitan Points of view

1. **Contemporary Workmanship and Writing**

   In the contemporary globalized world, different works of art and writing draw in with the mystery in assorted ways. Specialists and scholars frequently draw motivation from social customs, philosophical points of view, and the intricacies of current life. The puzzle turns into a material for communicating the vagueness and vulnerability intrinsic in the human experience.

2. **Innovative Puzzler**

The appearance of innovation has acquainted new aspects with the puzzler. Computerized reasoning, augmented experience, and the investigation of space suggest conversation starters that challenge how we might interpret presence. The mystery, in a mechanically determined society, reaches out past the regular and profound domains, raising moral issues and existential vulnerabilities.

XI. Union and Interconnectedness

As we study the horde ways various societies decipher and see the mystery, an example of interconnectedness arises. In spite of social variety, ongoing ideas can be found in the human propensity to look for significance, explore secret through ceremonies and imagery, and wrestle with the obscure in profound and philosophical pursuits.

The globalized universe of the 21st century offers an exceptional chance for social trade and blend. As individuals from different foundations come into contact, there is a rising acknowledgment of the wealth implanted in assorted points of view on the puzzle. This intercultural exchange can possibly cultivate a more comprehensive and comprehensive comprehension of the secrets that saturate human life.

The investigation of how various societies decipher and see the puzzle uncovers a kaleidoscope of points of view that improve how we might interpret the human experience. From the normal requests of Western way of thinking to the supernatural thoughts of Eastern practices, and the animistic associations in native societies, each social focal point gives a one of a kind vantage point.

As we cross the globe, we experience different scenes, conviction frameworks, and approaches to drawing in with the mystery. Whether through the otherworldly profundity of Sufism, the environmental familiarity with native practices, or the grandiose stories of old developments, the puzzler continues as a general string woven into the texture of humankind's shared mindset.

In our contemporary period, described by remarkable availability and mechanical headways, the puzzle takes on new aspects. As we explore the intricacies of a globalized world, the test is to appreciate and coordinate the insight implanted in different social viewpoints. In doing as such, we might find a more significant and agreeable approach to moving toward the conundrum, remembering it as a riddle to be settled as well as a consistently unfurling secret that welcomes persistent investigation and consideration.

The conundrum, as an idea, fills in as a captivating junction where different societies meet and veer in their understandings. From the judicious requests of old style Western way of thinking to the otherworldly hug of the obscure in Eastern practices, and the animistic association with nature in native societies, every point of view mirrors the extraordinary perspective of its social setting.

As the world turns out to be more interconnected, the trade and coordination of these different viewpoints add to a more extravagant and more nuanced comprehension of the puzzle. Whether moved toward through logical request, otherworldly investigation, or social relativism, the conundrum stays a dazzling and persevering through part of the human experience, welcoming us to consider the secrets that encompass us and shape the embroidery of our common presence.

www.ingramcontent.com/pod-product-compliance
Lightning Source LLC
Chambersburg PA
CBHW071205130726
47998CB00002B/618